Pr
Mindv

"This book evinces the intimate relationship between curiosity and creativity, mindwandering and mindfulness, agency and association, sentience and selfhood. It does so using a compelling mixture of personal narratives and high-end cognitive (and clinical) neuroscience; in which the author is wonderfully fluent (and internationally acclaimed). It is an addictive and eclectic read, crafted with a gentle and telling humor."

—KARL J. FRISTON, scientific director, Wellcome Centre for Human Neuroimaging; professor, University College London

"An important, entertaining, and instructive treatment. A gentle and humane book that should be read by everyone interested in the human mind and the human brain."

—ANDY CLARK, professor of cognitive philosophy, University of Sussex; author of *Surfing Uncertainty*

"A gold standard in neuroscience research is to prove links between brain activity and behavior. Bar's analysis of mindwandering offers us 'a good broad-ranging stroll' through all sorts of familiar human behaviors, provocatively locating them in relation to brain functions that he has spent decades studying. Highly accessible and entertaining, alternately personal and analytic, this lovely and stimulating book will make you appreciate your mind, and Bar's."

—SUSANNA SIEGEL, Edgar Pierce Professor of Philosophy, Harvard University

MOSHE BAR is the former Director of the Cognitive Neuroscience Lab at Harvard Medical School and Massachusetts General Hospital and an internationally renowned cognitive neuroscientist, whose novel research has made revolutionary contributions to our understanding of perception, cognition and issues in psychiatry. He has received many awards and honours, including the prestigious 21st Century Science Initiative Award from the McDonnell Foundation and the Hebb Award from the International Neural Networks Society. He now heads the Gonda Multidisciplinary Brain Research Center at Bar-Ilan University.

MINDWANDERING

How it can improve
your mood and boost
your creativity

Moshe Bar

BLOOMSBURY PUBLISHING
LONDON · OXFORD · NEW YORK · NEW DELHI · SYDNEY

BLOOMSBURY PUBLISHING
Bloomsbury Publishing Plc
50 Bedford Square, London, WC1B 3DP, UK
29 Earlsfort Terrace, Dublin 2, Ireland

BLOOMSBURY, BLOOMSBURY PUBLISHING and the Diana logo
are trademarks of Bloomsbury Publishing Plc

First published in 2022 in the United States by Hachette Go, an imprint of Hachette Books
First published in Great Britain 2022
This edition published 2023

A catalogue record for this book is available from the British Library

ISBN: HB: 978-1-4088-8805-6; TPB: 978-1-4088-8806-3; PB: 978-1-4088-8802-5;
eBook: 978-1-4088-8804-9; ePDF: 978-1-5266-5229-4

2 4 6 8 10 9 7 5 3 1

Interior design by Linda Mark
Printed and bound in Great Britain by CPI Group (UK) Ltd, Croydon CR0 4YY

MIX
Paper | Supporting
responsible forestry
FSC® C171272

To find out more about our authors and books visit
www.bloomsbury.com and sign up for our newsletters

For my parents, Hila and Avi

Contents

States of Mind

TALKING ABOUT SEX, KINK, AND ADHD, CATIE OSBORN, AN ACTOR AND a Shakespeare aficionado, confesses that before discovering the less conventional sexual practices of "kinkiness," her mind would often drift during sexual activities. In an interview for *Haaretz*, she says that discovering "kink" and BDSM was a purifying moment for her, helping her connect her mind with her body. When you are blindfolded and your partner slides an ice cube over your body, or drips hot wax on your skin, you stop thinking about the noise from the air conditioner or the squeaking of the bed. You are all immersed in the real thing. Indeed, extreme experiences drag you in by calling for your undivided attention. But once you've learned to give in and let the experience take you, it no longer needs to be reserved for extreme situations anymore. Imagine how your life could feel if eating a blueberry would be just as immersive as kink sex with hot wax on your skin, sucking in your entire mind. *Immersion* is a gift waiting inside our brain.

We all know how insistently mindwandering can hijack our attention, and as our lives have become so much more frenetic, people are increasingly worried about the quality of their mental experience; not just their ability to focus and get their work done, but their ability to enjoy their lives, to be truly, deeply engaged in them. I learned just how concerned they are when an op-ed I wrote, titled "Think Less, Think Better," was published by the *New York Times* a few years ago. In it I considered "how much we overlook, not just about the world, but also about the full potential of our inner life, when our mind is cluttered." As resonant as the piece was, it didn't touch on the important insights I have to share about why our minds wander and how their preoccupations are actually vital to our well-being even though some of our mindwandering is indeed harmful.

So much attention has been paid to ways to unplug from the bustle, and that's absolutely to be commended. I'll share my own positive experiences with doing so in silent meditation retreats. But as a series of discoveries in neuroscience over the past several decades have revealed, the greater challenge is freeing ourselves from the distractions within, which disrupt our attention and intrude on the quality of our experience even when we are in a perfectly quiet place. In fact, they may do so even more in times of quiet.

Research has revealed that our brains are inherently active. A number of brain regions connected in what's dubbed the default mode network (DMN) are always grinding away, engaged in a number of different involuntary activities that neuroscientists collectively call mindwandering: from daydreaming to the incessant self-chatter and from ruminating about the past to worrying about the future. The brain regions most often identified as being part of the DMN include the medial prefrontal cortex, the posterior cingulate cortex, and the angular gyrus, but there are several more that come and go as part of this massive, large-scale network. Not only does all of this inner commotion tug our attention away from the present moment, but it can dampen the quality of our experience, lowering our mood and potentially contributing to anxiety and depression. Yet there's a method to this apparent madness. Evolution has clearly taught our minds to wander. According to various studies, they're caught up in mindwandering between 30 and 47 percent of our waking time, gobbling up a great deal of energy.[1] The logic of evolution suggests there must be something beneficial about it, and over the course of the past couple of decades, I and my neuroscience compatriots have identified a core set of its important functions.

One line of research has shown that some of the default activity is concerned with developing our sense of self, through all sorts of cogitating and monitoring. Another line of research has found that a good amount of the DMN's activity is involved with assessing other people, which is dubbed Theory of Mind (ToM), trying to sort out what others are thinking and what they think of us.

As these findings began coming out, I was initially puzzled about how on earth my own discoveries about the DMN's activity fitted with these other functions. My research then focused on something quite different—visual cognition—and I found the DMN was highly involved in the process. I was trying to figure out how we piece together clues in the visual environment to construct an understanding of what we're seeing. In one such study, I would ask subjects to identify ambiguous objects that I had somewhat obscured in photos. As it turned out, if I showed them, say, a fuzzy image of a hairdryer in the setting of a bathroom, they would identify it as a hairdryer, but if I embedded the same fuzzy hairdryer image in the setting of a workbench, surrounded by a lot of tools, they would identify it as a drill.[2] I realized they were identifying objects by making associations between them and the things around them. Why would the same brain network involved in that associative activity also be engaged in developing a sense of self and Theory of Mind skills?

Then it came to me, like a bolt: all these mental processes involve making associations. Our sense of self, research has shown, is largely a form of prediction about who we are, about how we will think, feel, and behave in different situations, associating how we've thought, felt, and behaved in similar situations in the past with how we will do so now and in the future. The same is true for how we develop our assessments of others. Associations are the building blocks of most mental operations.

This is, essentially, why so much of the DMN's mindwandering activity is concerned with thinking about the past and the future, taking us away from the now. We're searching memory for associations to help us interpret what's happening in our lives and what might be coming. We're intently making all manner of predictions. Indeed, as I continued researching what people were thinking about when their DMN was active, I found that they're often creating elaborate scenarios of future events, like little movies about how situations in their lives are going to play out. No wonder so much of our mental energy is hogged by the DMN. After all, knowing how to interpret situations, establishing a sense of who we are, understanding others as best we can, and anticipating what turn of events we might need to be prepared for are all crucial to making our way through life.

The problem is that we can become so engaged in this consideration of the past and making predictions, and so reliant on associations that we've made based on experience, that for much of the time, we're disconnected from what's actually happening in the moment. This not only interferes with our focus but also leads to all sorts of misinterpretations that cause problems in our lives, such as when we mistakenly think someone is untrustworthy because they remind us of someone else who was. Or we might experience unnecessary anxiety that we're going to be laid off because our boss is acting in a way we associate, incorrectly, with displeasure in us. A preoccupation with the past and the future also leads us to lose some of our ability to perceive novelty. We're so inclined to perceive expected associations that we overlook unexpected connections, which stunts both discovery and creativity.

As I contemplated all of these findings about the DMN and mind-wandering, I came to what for me has been a groundbreaking realization. We don't want to just clamp down on all mindwandering, which is just as well because that's virtually impossible. What we want to do instead is become more aware of when and how our minds are wandering. Then we can become more effective at directing that activity voluntarily as much as possible, so we can buckle down and focus on tasks or, alternatively, let ourselves be truly, deeply immersed in the experience of the moment. At other times, when we want to stimulate our creativity, as well as our mood, we'll do best to free our minds to indulge in a good broad-ranging stroll. We want, in short, to work toward being able to bring the right mind to the right time.

Vital to building up our ability to do this is the understanding that so much of our mindwandering is aimed at helping us exploit our memories of past experiences, to assist us in figuring out how to solve problems at work or in our lives, drawing our attention inward. But in my lab, I found that we could induce a broadly associative type of mindwandering that is exploratory, ranging all over and open to novel perceptions. This type of mindwandering is like the polar opposite of rumination, which is narrowly focused on some memory or worry. And because I had read that rumination dampens mood, I decided to conduct studies to see if when our minds are engaged in this type of broad, exploratory mindwandering, our mood is lifted. Yes, it is! By merely reading chains of words that expand broadly, like the chain "wolf–moon–dark side–Pink Floyd–*The Wall*–Germany–EU," our mood becomes significantly more positive. This finding is as groundbreaking as it is simple to explain, and we currently use it to alleviate symptoms associated with depression, anxiety, and stress. Then we decided to see if when we improve people's mood, their minds would also begin engaging in broader-ranging mindwandering. They did! How astonishing: the causal connection goes both ways. This led us to conjecture that if people's mood was lifted, and they were engaging in broader-ranging mindwandering, they would also be more creative in providing solutions to tasks we assigned them. They were! These findings were thrilling, and they led me, through steps I'll narrate here, to the realization that our brains are constantly moving along a continuum between two fundamental, and opposing, states of mind, which I call exploratory and exploitatory, and the degree to which our mind is wandering and in what ways will dramatically differ in each.

IN THE EXPLORATORY STATE, OUR MINDS ARE OPEN TO NOVEL INFORMATION— experiencing and observing the moment, willing to stomach some uncertainty for the benefit of learning—our creativity is stoked, and we're in a relatively upbeat mood. If our minds are wandering, they'll be doing so in an enjoyable, free-ranging way. In the exploitatory state, on the other hand, we're focused on drawing from our past experience, relying on tried-and-true methods for interpreting the situation and for solving problems, preferring the certainty of the familiar over the thrill of the new, and our mood will be comparatively dampened. If our minds are wandering, they'll be doing so in a relatively narrow way. The exploratory is outward focused, bottom-up, and experiential, while the exploitatory is inward oriented, top-down, and procedural. Our minds are never really at one or the other extreme, but they will tend to favor more of one versus the other at any given moment.

The exploratory state sure sounds far more fun, but both are vital for our success and our well-being. The key is that as we go about any given task or experience, as much as we can, we want to muster the state of mind (SoM) that's optimal for the specific situation. And if we're on a vacation with our kids, we want to be in bottom-up, broad experiential mode as much as we can, fully enjoying the moments with them, not pulled constantly into mindwandering about our work or old mental templates. If we've got to get a report written by tomorrow morning, we want to be in top-down, narrowly focused mode. If we're searching for a big new idea—say, for a product to create—we want to be in broadly associative mindwandering mode.

A lot has been discovered and said already about how flexible our brains are. This is the key to our evolution and to our survival in most circumstances, and we are lucky for having such an elastic, open-minded brain. There is certainly no magical formula for gaining control over our mental state, but I have found that by being aware of the need to try to calibrate my state of mind on this exploratory/exploitatory continuum for the situation I'm in, I'm increasingly able to do so. I aimed to replicate here the exhilarating intellectual journey I and my neuroscience colleagues have traveled in making these findings. But I do also want to share some insights about building up more ability to put our minds in the state we'd like them in. Some of these insights are organized and collated in the Appendix, and while they are not provided here as overly concrete prescriptions, applying them in everyday life could be a personal quest of discovery and adjustments.

One great help for me has been mindfulness meditation, and I'll share here how my experiences at silence retreats have helped me build up my awareness of my state of mind and purposefully nudge it the way I want it to go. But I'll also discuss how meditation, and developing a high degree of mindfulness, has limits when it comes to optimizing our mental state, not the least of which is that so many people find mindfulness training unpleasant. My research illuminates one reason for this. Meditation is an extremely narrow form of mental activity—the antithesis of broadly associative mindwandering—so it makes sense that it can be unenjoyable in some respects. In addition, mindfulness, if we were to rigorously impose it on ourselves constantly, would turn us into observers of our lives, making it harder to be fully engaged in the living of them, to be lost in the rush of experience. While mindfulness offers numerous advantages, and I recommend that all human beings at least give it a try, we very much want to have some of that utterly immersed-in-the-moment time in our lives.

As much as I've been gaining more control, my mind still wanders at plenty of times I don't want it to. Our minds always will to some extent. One of the biggest takeaways for me from my work on mindwandering is that I'm less stressed about that, because I know why it's going on. Just the other day, I took a professor visiting from Stanford, whose work and personality I greatly admire, for lunch in a Tel Aviv café. At some point in our conversation, he told me he had once heard something that had completely changed him, how he thinks and how he lives his life, and he wanted to share it with me. I have no idea what it was. Even in spite of that dramatic introduction, my mind drifted far away as he spoke, and I was too embarrassed once I realized what had happened to tell him I hadn't caught what he'd said. I can only imagine how odd he must have thought it was that I didn't comment meaningfully about his revelation. Instead, I quickly changed the subject. Happily, though, I can report that my mind had wandered to something interesting in my own life. Perverse as our mindwandering can be, at least it generally does have a purpose.

CHAPTER ONE

ALWAYS "ON"

MUCH OF NEUROSCIENCE RESEARCH UP TO THE DEVELOPMENT OF BRAIN scanning was somewhat akin to phrenology, the Victorian practice of inferring people's mental character by feeling the shape of their skulls. Of course, I'm overstating the case, but in studying the internal workings of the brain, the assumption for a long time has been that different areas within the brain would be dedicated to different tasks: one for language, another for memory; one for recognizing faces, another for feeling emotions. Over time, however, we came to realize that the operation and architecture of the brain are much more distributed over large networks than being modular and compartmentalized. Most, if not all, functions are accomplished via the activation and orchestration of multiarea networks. No single region, let alone individual neurons, accomplishes much without short- and long-distance cooperation. And in the context of mindwandering and the brain's default network that mediates it, it is worth noting that different states of mind, such as meditation and sleep, as well as different psychiatric conditions all affect not only the information content in this massive network, but also the extent of connectivity between the cortical nodes of this network. The different areas constituting the network could be more strongly or more weakly connected in different states, more or less synchronized with each other, and influence each other to different degrees. Now we know that the brain is broadly dynamic and flexible in its operation and in its characteristics.

Still, we are far from a solid understanding of even the most basic neural functions. I learned this with a shock as a student in the laboratory of Professor Shimon Ullman, a pioneer in the development of computer vision. At the time, I was just finishing studying electrical engineering, out of an ill-conceived notion of fulfilling my father's ambitions for me to be an engineer. I had quickly learned that I had absolutely no interest in chip design and that the only area of research in the field that captivated me was computer vision. The aim of this field was to mimic the way the human brain represents and recognizes images, and I discovered that at that time, thirty years ago, no one had a clear idea of how it is accomplished. I found that outrageous, and with the zeal of a young student with a whole lot yet to learn, I told Ullman so. He responded, as I recall, that I'd soon come to appreciate how complex the workings of the brain are. That I did. Sadly, it is still largely true that we have no hard knowledge of how the brain recognizes images, mainly some intriguing theories with preliminary support.

Fortunately, during my work in his lab, and then much more extensively in the cognitive psychology lab of another pioneer, Irv Biederman, a door was opened to a more productive, and exciting, new area of research that had just gotten under way, which I left to pursue. A major new way for studying the brain had recently been invented:

fMRI (functional magnetic resonance imaging). The MRI machine it-self, which uses magnetic fields and radio-frequency waves to image the anatomy of biological tissues, bones, and body organs, had been around for a few decades at that point, mostly in use in medical contexts. But the *f*, functional, MRI was the breakthrough neuroscientists had been thirsty for. By measuring blood flow, the functional part of fMRI allows us to infer where and when brain activity takes place. Maps of brain activity could be created by "sticking subjects in the magnet" and ask-ing them to look at pictures, listen to sounds, count sheep—all sorts of tasks. We could look into the human brain during its normal, ongoing operation. Of course, that is with a few caveats, such as that what is measured is not exactly brain activation but rather a proxy, and that even interpretations of data can be subjective, but a revolution never-theless. This was a moment of extraordinary adventure; we were roam-ing around inside the pathways of the mind like hikers in the woods at night with flashlights. And we soon stumbled upon the first truly substantial finding through neuroimaging.

The Discovery of the Brain's Default Mode Network

Excited by the explosion of research, I got myself to Harvard Medical School, where Ken Kwong, Bruce Rosen, and collaborators were doing some of the most important work. My timing was fortuitous. A momen-tous discovery had recently been made: neuroimaging had paved the way to the discovery of the brain's default mode and of the prevalence of mindwandering in everyday life.

What made the advent of fMRI so groundbreaking is that we no longer had to compromise on analogies to animals' brains, we no longer had to make do with postmortem brains, we no longer had to infer the operation of the healthy brain from head and brain injuries (like that of the famous Phineas Gage or gunshot injuries in the Spanish Civil War), and we no longer had to limit ourselves to whatever can be recorded from patients during (or prior to) brain surgery. The result is beautifully colorful images that are taken as neural activation maps.

What are those colorful brain activations we see in fMRI studies? They are typically the result of a subtraction between what is evoked in the brain by two different experimental conditions. Imagine there is a study about emotional processing, specifically looking at what happens in the brain when we see happy faces compared with what happens in the brain when looking at sad faces. A participant (a "subject") is asked to lie still on the sliding MRI bed—with a big cage (radio-frequency coil) around her head, loud high-frequency noises from the machine, in cold temperature—and attend what is projected to her on the screen. The fMRI signal is measured for each and every presentation trial. The brain activity elicited by all trials of one condition (all the happy faces) is averaged together and is subtracted from the average activation elicited by the trials of the other condition (all the sad faces). The resulting map shows areas where one condition activated more strongly (usually warm red-yellow colors) and less strongly (usually cold bluish colors) than the other condition. So, in our example, brain areas that show red are those where happy faces elicited stronger neuronal activity than sad faces, and blue spots correspond to regions where the sad faces activated more strongly than happy faces. And these maps are used to try to infer something new about the underlying neuronal mechanisms.

In between the experimental conditions (sad and happy faces in our example), there is a short rest period, usually a blank screen or a screen with a fixation dot at the center. This is used both for recovering the MRI signal for analysis purposes as well as to provide the participants with some rest in between experimental blocks of trials. And here comes the critical thing: While no one really believed that the brain is silent and inactive during those rest periods, the implicit assumption had been that it is much less active when our participants are resting and not required to perform any demanding task. The revolutionary discovery happened when, serendipitously looking at the activation maps during those rest periods, researchers started to notice that the brain is actually vigorously active when there is no specific task to perform, often more intensely than during the experimental conditions themselves, in a highly reliable manner, and in an extensive network, the DMN.

This accidental discovery of the DMN is most often attributed to Marcus Raichle and his coworkers, though the work was conducted by many labs.[1] This network has since been dubbed the default network, this activity the default activity, and this state the brain's default mode. Since its discovery, this default network has been readily found and replicated across many laboratories, paradigms, and MRI machines. By now it is accepted as a solid finding.

With all the excitement surrounding the early years of fMRI, it is clear now that what it measures and what is reported are not direct activations and not always consistent. There are many stages where distortion might creep in: from the moment we neuroscientists design an experiment to running it in machines that vary in sensitivities, with tens of parameters that could each change from one experiment to the next, to the analysis stage where there are numerous possible approaches with different strengths and weaknesses, to the limit of our interpretations. Indeed, the peak of the healthy skepticism regarding fMRI research matured in a recent study showing that when seventy different independent groups analyzed the exact same data set, they reported different results.[2] While this is good to keep in mind as we are being exposed to more and more neuroimaging studies and subsequent claims, it is much less a concern in our context here. No one contests the existence and general behavior of the DMN. It is gigantic, it is omnipresent, and it is exceptionally replicable. We can proceed with our effort to understand the function(s) and characteristics of the brain's default mode network.

The discovery of the DMN was sensational. Neural activity is highly energy consuming. Why would our brains waste so much metabolic energy when they were presumably doing nothing? When I arrived at Harvard as a postdoc, research had just commenced to determine what the function of the DMN might be. Using the intriguing method of thought sampling, combined with brain imaging, we learned that the more active the DMN is, the more one's brain is engaged in mindwandering. It took the next couple of decades for the community to work out various important functions this seemingly spontaneous activity serves, with several different lines of research evolving.

As I grew as a neuroscientist, I came to develop two maxims about this fascinating research. The first is that evolution does not make mistakes. Everything we see in the brain has a reason and a function. Illusions, various "blindnesses," cell suicide, false memories, and other findings that are puzzling and sometimes also amusing tend to make people believe they just caught the brain misbehaving, only to later realize these are various reflections of a grander strength. For the brain to be so flexible, adaptable, agile, and efficient, it has to pay some prices. (Indeed, when I am being asked why artificial intelligence algorithms do not behave like the human brains that they try to imitate, my answer is that AI is still more engineering than neuroscience. By making a computer perform a task with rigid boundaries of how to achieve goals, and with little accommodation for exceptions and improvisation, the artificial system lacks more implicit but immensely critical aspects of the human brain, such as flexibility and ingenuity.) So, in our context, once we realize that the brain is vigorously active when we are not busy with a specific goal, like when waiting in line, standing in the shower, or listening to something boring, knowing that this activity consumes significant energy should tell us that this activity must play some important role.

The second maxim, one that started in the mind of a young and naive postdoc but still serves me to this day, is that the brain always tells you, the inquisitive scientist, the truth. When things do not make sense, it is because you are not asking the right question or you are not asking the right question properly. The brain typically does not volunteer information, but the answers are there, waiting for us to arrive.

A relentless brain, always "on," what does it do when we are not busy? The chapters ahead will tell the story of that often perplexing but always thrilling path of discovery and how findings that seemed quite disparate have been coming together. But before delving into this journey of unveiling the purpose of the DMN and of mindwandering, let us first give our thoughts a serious examination.

CHAPTER TWO

CONNECTING WITH OUR THOUGHTS

W E DO NOT THINK ABOUT OUR THOUGHTS OFTEN ENOUGH, BUT thoughts are the building blocks of our mental life, and of mindwandering. Thoughts are how we get from one idea to the next. They can be verbal, visual, and more; they can be progressing fast or slow; they can span many different semantic topics; they are based on stuff we know and have stored in memory; they can be of varying emotional valance; and they are often manifested as an internal dialogue between me and I. Thoughts are the interface and the translation of our inner world to our conscious mind, which can then be communicated to the outside world, or just remain with us.

The Source of Our Thoughts

When thoughts are aimed at a specific goal, they follow an agenda and a clear structure, not predictable, but nevertheless with a coherent progression, like when solving a problem. They accumulate and advance toward that goal. Planning is a good example. There is a chair at home you wanted to fix yourself, and you are thinking of doing it tomorrow morning. You think of the stuff you need to gather, like glue, a dead-blow hammer, a scrub plane, a wood chisel, a saw, and a sanding block. You "travel" along the web of concepts you have in memory, and you pick up the items that are relevant and necessary. You realize you need new protective gloves, so you think you will first go buy a new pair. You are thinking of where you will be doing the work exactly, the order of steps required for the repair, a complete simulation of what you are going to do to bring the chair back to function, how you are going to do this after everyone has left the house, and what your daughter's reaction will be when she comes back to see her favorite chair fixed. That's a train with a beginning and an end.

Sometimes we are more associative and more easily distracted, so when you get to the chisel in our list above, you diverge to thinking about Geppetto and Pinocchio and about a growing nose, and lying, and then you recall how your son told you he lied about having taken the dog out for a walk because he was lazy but too embarrassed to admit it. Then you think about how lucky you are to have this dog (and this son); you think about his playful attitude and how he lifts your spirits every day when you come back home. And you never get back to that fix-that-chair train.

We actually have one long train of thought during our waking hours. It changes topics, speed, style, orientation, content, and other characteristics, but it is continuous; there are no real pauses in thinking.

The source of our thoughts and what determines our next thought is a subject of developing and ongoing investigation. We all possess a sense of total agency over our thoughts, but this sense is unfounded. Conscious and subconscious thoughts mix, interact, exchange, and trigger processes in each other. We feel that we are privy to our thoughts and that if you asked us, we would know to tell you where our thoughts have originated and how one thought is connected to the one before and the one after. We believe that we are the owners and monitors of our thoughts, but this sense of agency is naive. You walk down the street thinking about an article you read last night, and suddenly you find yourself thinking about your high school teacher whom you have not seen for many years and who has no apparent connection to anything that was going through your mind a second ago. Our false sense of agency means that most of us, most of the time, cannot accept that the thought was triggered by a source unbeknownst to our conscious self. So we fabricate a link instead or just believe it popped up in our mind spontaneously.

But there is no such thing; thoughts do not just pop up. Each thought is connected to something, only sometimes this connection is beyond our conscious reach. That thoughts are connected does not mean that the thought process is always coherent, logically leading from one to the next. Interruptions to trains of thought could come from outside stimuli, like the sound of breaking glass or someone calling our name, or from an internal process, such as reminiscing on something emotional, and we can be aware of that interruption or not. Something on that street on which you were walking triggered the memory of your high school teacher, like somebody wearing distinct glasses like your teacher used to wear, but you could not trace back what that cue was. Perhaps it was because your eyes moved too quickly over that cue for the trigger to register in your conscious awareness or because you saw (or heard or smelled) something that you did not know in your mind was associated with your teacher. So now you are thinking about her without intending to and without understanding why, but your mind still follows that path.

Now let's consider the path that our thoughts take even in a vacuum, with no interruptions whatsoever. Imagine the giant web that is your memory, with names, objects, places, concepts, and feelings all connected through associations. The thought process involves metaphorically walking on this web, from one node to the next, to transition from one concept node, or idea, to another. Every point in your path is connected to the previous one and to the next one, even if you cannot see it in every step. It is a web, so in every node you typically can go in multiple directions, and your mind chooses one. Let's say you think that you need a vacation. When you stand on the "vacation" node of your web of possible thoughts, you could move on to the "money" branch and develop the financial consequences of going on vacation; you could go on the "fun" branch and start with happy mental simulations; or you could go in the direction of concrete planning of the right time and right destination for the vacation. With every step you take, your mind has to choose the next step out of several possibilities. Not consciously, and not with much deliberation, but it does. What determines the next step in your chain of thought is a little tug-of-war between different sources pulling you in different directions, and only one wins: your personality (frugal or not, open to new experience or not), state of mind, dispositions, the recent history of your thoughts (if you just paid the bills an hour ago you are more likely to go the "money" path, but if you just watched a commercial of a vacation on a beautiful island you will go on the "fun" path instead, owing to a phenomenon we call "priming"), or deep subconscious forces that draw you to the "I've got to get away from all this" path all compete for your selection.

While each node in our web of concepts and memories is connected to multiple other nodes at once, these connections are not of equal strength. Connections between neurons have "weights" that stand for the strength of their association. The strength between A and B determines how likely, how easily, and how quickly thought A will activate thought B, so when you see or think A, you will next think B. The strength of these weights may be determined by the quality of learning, such as how rehearsed this link is (how often a red light means "stop"), or could be temporary and determined dynamically by previous mental events that may keep a certain association primed.

Not knowing that activations of thoughts come from deterministic sources—be it priming by history, subconscious forces, or strength of association—can result, and does result, in many everyday confusions, not only our false belief in total agency over our thoughts and the illusion of free will that comes with it. Free association has been a major therapeutic tool since Freud and Jung and has proven potent in its capacity to unveil thoughts that are hidden from the individual's conscious access. In the free-association method, the participant is presented with a word and encouraged to respond as quickly as possible with the first thing that comes to her mind, without censorship and without being judged. The idea is that under encouraging and nonintimidating conditions, inhibition is minimized and the things that then emerge from the freely associative responses are informative about the individual's inner workings, deep desires, hidden fears, and surprising urges. But one needs to keep in mind the other sources that determine our next thought, as listed above, when trying to understand why I said or why I thought what I just did. If your therapist says "mother" and you respond with "blood," she will be alarmed about your possible relationship with your mom. It could be a justified concern by your therapist, but another possible source for your response might be that you called your mom this morning to ask how to remove a bloodstain from your shirt and the semantic concept "blood" was thus primed, or warmed up, and therefore more readily provided as your quick response. We need to understand why thought A led to thought B before we can draw meaningful conclusions.

Observing Thoughts

My first formal adventure into my own inner world started by registering for a short course of mindfulness (mindfulness-based stress reduction, or MBSR, eight evenings and one final day of silence). There was a preliminary meeting to handle logistics such as paperwork and info on what to bring to the actual meetings. It was in Amherst, Massachusetts, where Jon Kabat-Zinn had fortunately distilled mindfulness meditation for the masses, and for this organizational meeting all groups were seated together in a giant circle on a basketball court. Just before standing up to leave, the instructors asked us to relax and close our eyes for one silent minute and then to share the experience with the others. It seemed like a benign, almost infantile, exercise. But this little minute opened a new world for me. The sudden pause, the radical change of my mental orientation inward, the long-forgotten sensation and attention to my own body struck me instantaneously. My life around that time was extremely hectic, being a young faculty in the competitive Harvard environment, with little kids at home, and more. When was the last time I had felt like that, I asked myself, and why had I not stopped for just one personal minute for so long? This is just like the clichéd question of when was the last time you looked up at the stars. Only this cosmos was inside of me, intense, personal, and waiting. I wanted to go deeper, and although it took me a few years to take that step, it paid off.

That I was encouraged to "observe" my thoughts initially sounded like complete nonsense. But I had made a decision before enrolling to suspend skepticism, to leave my scientist hat back home, and to come tabula rasa. So, I gave in and tried. We can observe ourselves in the mirror, notice a new wrinkle, focus on it for a little bit, and move on: observe, notice, examine, and let go. There is no real reason we would not be able to do the same thing inwardly on our thoughts. It is amazing how interesting, how accessible, and how intimate this experience can be, yet most of us do not venture in this direction our entire life.

We grew to see our thought process as impervious to personal examination. My first experience of silence, even as a (largely undisciplined) beginner, gave me the unequivocal realization that I had found a personal gold mine. Focusing on my thoughts very quickly started to seem like performing a sort of psychoanalysis on myself. Initially, you are occupied by mundane thoughts of what bothered you last: your trip over, things you left behind at home and at work, things you need and want to do after you are done, the smell in the room, or a distant sound. Then you start delving into older issues, memories, fears, and desires. You may find yourself smiling, or crying, with the sheer power of thinking inwardly. Strong emotions can be evoked simply by wading through our memories. And all this, I now know, can happen to you regardless of the mechanics of the meditation practice. The mere awareness that you are able and can benefit from looking into your mental being as a curious observer can then allow it to also take place during your everyday life, while making a salad or while jogging, and it does not require a special apparatus, clothing, or environment. The simple understanding that it is possible for me to look at my own thoughts has helped me gain a better notion of what bothers me, what makes me happy, why I say what I say, do what I do, feel what I feel, and behave like myself. That said, meditation can also expose thoughts and memories that you have been avoiding for a reason or that you do not yet have the skills to cope with and could use external help, so it is not a practice that is exclusively constructive.

I am obviously not the first one to stumble upon this fountain of observations about the self. Centuries of spiritual practices, psychological examinations, and even self-discoveries by many have preceded me. One that I would like to single out is Marion Milner (or Joanna Field, her pseudonym), who has gone long and far by keeping a meticulous and richly insightful diary when she decided to follow her experiences in a quest to find happiness. This eight-year journey is summarized exquisitely in her book *A Life of One's Own*.[1] Through her diary keeping, Milner developed a unique mastery of introspection. It is no wonder that she later became an established psychoanalyst.

We are used to being the subjects of our thoughts, being inside our train of thoughts, right at the center, almost as if our thoughts operate on us, with minimal control or insight of how and where they go. But this new practice of mine, and of many before me, means adding a vantage point of observing one's own thoughts from the side. And this practice is really no art or something with which one needs tens of thousands of hours of experience before harvesting the benefits. It is merely an effort for a change of perspective. There are two possible perspectives: either you are inside your thoughts and experiencing them like a person sitting on a roller coaster, or you are observing them like someone who has not bought a ticket and is looking at the roller coaster from the ground. These two modes can then alternate, switching from immersive participation to outside observation, either automatically or at will. After a while it feels seamless to shift between them.

Integrating personal experience of observing thoughts with our progressive understanding of the mind (psychology) and the brain (neuroscience) allows a new and accessible grasp of who and why we are.

Thoughts and Mental Noise

In the world of engineering and signal processing, there is a measure termed signal-to-noise ratio (SNR). It quantifies how much a signal of interest is embedded within an otherwise noisy environment. Most realistic environments are incredibly noisy: radio reception in an environment filled with many other radio transmissions; visual images of the scene around us are crowded with clutter, obstructions, motions, varying illuminations, and more; and cocktail parties, where you have to fight distracting sounds and chatter to be able to understand what your friend is saying. A good system is one that amplifies the signal and suppresses the noise, maximizing SNR, so that you get what is interesting. The brain has to tackle the same issue, in considering both the external as well as the internal worlds.

For the external signals of interest, how we consume our physical environment is filtered by attention, an ingenious screen that allows us to select, not necessarily consciously, only the things that are relevant, novel, attractive, or scary. We are constantly bombarded with a wealth of physical stimulation, like sounds, colors, smells, and more. Say you are on a busy street, waiting for your bus, when there is one approaching from the distance and you need to know if this is your bus. Think how much information you would have to discard to be able to focus: cars near the bus, objects in your periphery, motion signals that emanate from the hustle and bustle of a busy street, distracting honking, the weight of your bags, the conversation going on in the background, and much more. Yet we usually have no problem going around our lives while ignoring the vast majority of our environment. This sometimes leads to interesting and often amusing cases of missing important aspects of our surroundings, like the "invisible gorilla" test where people who count basketball passes with intense concentration miss a gorilla passing the scene from side to side (originally demonstrated by Ulric Neisser, one of the founding fathers of cognitive psychology).[2] But by and large, selective attention is a powerful gift of nature that keeps us safe, sane, and efficient.

We can also think of attention as applied inwardly. We can be attentive to certain thoughts and not others (thought suppression/repression notwithstanding), and the practice of meditation is the most effective tool I know to do so. You can think of meditation as reducing mental noise, thereby amplifying the SNR of your thoughts. And it gives you the sublime power not only to understand your thoughts, but also to exert at least some control over them. Would you sit in a car that drives by itself anywhere it desires? No. So why would you agree to live in a body where you are not at the helm?

We clean and improve SNR, and we then handle remaining thoughts gingerly, like visitors, as they are called sometimes: we observe them and label them, and next is silence, silence that allows mindfulness to flourish, to experience our world as close to how it really is as possible. Meditation lets us take control of our mind, while distilling thoughts. It also gets us closer to our insights.

What is the link between a quieter mind and connecting with our insights? Psychological studies of insight in problem solving and other cognitive feats show that insights are usually abrupt and appear unannounced. They behave like the result of unconscious processing, such as what we call "incubation." They are the processes that take place "behind the scenes" of our conscious mind, taking care of mental tasks without bothering us when it is not necessary. An insight is our unconscious mind transmitting to our conscious mind the final outcome of that incubation process. It is like we hire a subcontractor to do work for us when we do not care about the details, so we can continue with our lives in the meantime. We need to be ready to receive those messages once they are transmitted, but it is hard for an occupied conscious mind to notice little messages broadcast to it from within the depth of the sub-conscious. Thoughts hijack our mind, and there is too much noise to notice insights embedded within thoughts. By cleaning up background thoughts, increasing signal-to-noise ratio, meditation makes us open for more. These are the same mechanisms for being mindful of our internal as our external environments, with similar practices and similar benefits.

When practicing meditation, you become mindful not only of your thoughts, but even more so of your emotions, especially those that make you divert attention from the breathing: desire and longing, craving for a different experience, anger, criticism, judgment, anxiety, fear, restless-ness, tiredness, numbness, and doubt. But not to worry, it is not only negative emotions and thoughts that arise.

Often, especially at the beginning, I would find myself not able to concentrate in a group setting, and I would open my eyes. It is a curious sight in its own right. A group of people, strangers, all sit straight, with their eyes closed, surrounded by colorful pillows, shawls, and whatever makes them comfortable, silent, clearly not asleep but also not awake, and somehow their faces have that unique expression of being drawn and absorbed inwardly. It is something you would rarely see in any other setting. They all look so intimate with themselves that I have to admit it seemed a bit forbidden to be staring at them when they are having such personal experiences. But these occasional peeks showed me the range of emotions people experience while looking inside, with no external stimulation.

Breathing and Thinking

I once was invited to give a talk in beautiful Assisi, Italy. I landed in Rome, and a local friend and her husband picked me up from the airport. It was all planned so that I would arrive on time to meet my host, Patrizio, a kind Renaissance man who was interested in Buddhism and in doing good, just before a meditation retreat he was running in the woods around Assisi. My flight had arrived late, so we needed to rush. There was a three-hour drive ahead of us, and we hardly had time to stop for a quick lunch. The only topic of discussion throughout the drive was would we or would we not make it on time. Everything was rushed, and I felt like a character in a thriller movie: changing cars along the way, giving my luggage to the husband while the friend continued with me in another car, parking, running to meet the host in the nick of time. I shook his hand, breathless from the intense journey, but feeling like I had just saved the planet. And he, calm as anyone could be, tells me, "Come join us. We are going to sit for four hours now while focusing on the breath and the philtrum," pointing at the vertical groove between the upper lip and the bottom of the nose. Rushing only rarely pays off.

There are numerous methods for cleaning and sharpening your mind through meditation; not all are so intense or tedious. There is the famous mantra meditation, which I have never tried myself but seems to be pretty popular. There is the basic and friendly method of body scanning, which was my first experience ever. You sit, lie, or stand, close your eyes, and scan your body in your mind's eye in high detail. The space between your toes and underneath your nails, you go up from there and try to cover every point in your body with your imagination. Never in my experience have I managed to make it all the way to the top of my head, and that's okay; as the soft-spoken instructors tell you, the mind wanders, and you should not resist. You simply bring your attention back to scanning your body.

You can also meditate standing, while slowly and meticulously examining sensations on your feet with intricate resolution. And you can also meditate while walking, very slowly. You focus on the little movements of your body, your feet, your toes, your knees, your muscles, the posture of your head, and so forth. I found this one the hardest. Perhaps symbolizing my way of living, walking for me is associated with getting somewhere, not walking simply for the sake of walking. So, walking slowly does not make sense for my body, which has been living in a rush to arrive for so long. Unconditioning what has been conditioned over a lifetime requires practice.

The focus of your attention does not necessarily have to be your body. It could be examining a nearby air conditioner in detail, for that matter. Choosing a grounding object to which to return every time your mind wanders is a "head fake." It is the base method to help you train your mind to observe and slowly minimize distractions. To notice distractions, you need to be distracted from something. In meditation, that something is your grounding object, be it your body or whatever. In real life, what you are distracted from is the present.

The most popular approach, and it seems for very good reasons, is attending your breath. If you have no experience with meditation, I know well how this sounds to you. "What's there to attend in your breath, only air coming in and out? How long can one think about such a mundane and simple operation?" But the longer you practice, and the more extensive your instruction is, the finer is the resolution of your attention. Gradually, you start noticing the flow of air through your nostrils. Is it warm? Does it tickle? Is it slow and long or intense but short? You start attending the path of the air from your nose and mouth to your lungs and back out. Is it affected by your posture, your abdominal muscles? In and out: When does one breath end and the next one begin?

It is intriguing how any target you choose can become so infinitely detailed merely by attending it. We go about our lives seeing things as complete entities, closed objects, to which we attach names: a house, a tree, a person, a city, the moon. The same goes for our ability to imagine and bring up information to our mind's eye. If you close your eyes and think of your car, or your cat, or your office, unless you dwell and attend in detail, you see only rudimentary information. But what happens if you pause for a couple of minutes to focus on that tree you were about to walk by mindlessly? Suddenly, the tree has a trunk, bark, branches, twigs, leaves, buds, veins on leaves, colors, little flowers. It is like those fractal animations that when you go in, you reveal new fractals, endlessly. Merely dwelling is sufficient for a constant flow of more details, layer after layer.

My friend Nataly, who has been practicing yoga and meditation seriously for a long time, told me about a uniquely challenging exercise she received in one of her courses: to observe her breath closely for an entire day, while going about her activities. I can't imagine myself reaching this stage soon, but it sounds like an intriguing experience. This is how I learned from her a new term, "the real time." We all know how time feels subjectively to pass differently in different circumstances—slow when bored and fast when having fun, for example. Yet it seems that a prolonged and intense meditation can bring about a more stable perception of time, where subjective biases are minimized. The real time is the only time that matters.

Thoughts on Bodily Sensations

I remember running after the head of my first silence retreat, the founder of that Vipassana Tovana organization in Israel, Stephen Fulder, trying to tell him I was not feeling anything. Only one day had passed, but I am the impatient type, eager for insights. In fact, I was so curious and anxious that I was willing to talk in a silence retreat, also putting Stephen in an awkward position. But he got over it and told me to start by noticing how different thoughts that arose during the sittings affected my body. I did not understand what he meant. "Do you mean thoughts affect my body, and different thoughts affect my body differently?" He smiled and said, "Sure. You are a neuroscientist. For you there is only the brain." And he was right. Until that experience, the body in my very selective eyes was pretty much a platform for carrying the brain. In the superb and original film *The City of Lost Children*, where a scientist kidnaps children to harvest their dreams so he can stay young, Uncle Irvin is merely a brain in a jar, which does not stop him from being talkative and obnoxiously sarcastic and even to suffer from migraines. That is pretty much how I had been considering our being: it starts and ends in the brain.

In neuroscience, philosophy, Buddhism, and religious studies, people have been pondering the interaction between mind and body for ages. There is no question that we feel our body in our brain; there is plenty of evidence for that. But it is not yet common knowledge that this relationship is reciprocal. The body is much more than conveying sensory information to our brains, whether we are approaching something hot or we are being pleasantly tickled. In fact, several studies already suggest that our mind is shaped by signals from the body.[3] So it seems like a symbiotic connection that should be recognized and remembered.

One good example for the mind-body connection is the omnipresent phenomenon of placebo, where your beliefs and expectations can affect your physiological health. Both in the clinical world as well as in our everyday life, beliefs can change the way we respond to events, to the extent that we even change, unconsciously, pathological, psychological, and physiological symptoms. Proper context and instructions make even inert treatment effective. For example, at least 30 percent of depression cases can be alleviated by placebo,[4] which means that the depressive condition can be improved by the belief in therapy independent of the therapy itself. Similarly, placebo has been shown to alleviate symptoms of migraines and help manage pain in diverse domains.[5] It is the power of our mind over our mind and over our body.

Once I was giving a presentation in my daughter's kindergarten, and I asked the little kids where happiness was in the body as well as sadness, and jealousy, and anger. They responded with "brain" to all of them, except for love; love was in the "heart," they said. You feel your heart pounding, and our early intuition is that where you feel it is where it resides. This must be why in older times it was harder to suspect that all the human repertoire of feelings is happening inside the head. When there is not yet knowledge about the brain, and the only things that can be observed are the sensations in the body, that is where you would suspect they take place. And it makes a lot of sense that we would develop like that. If your right toe is the part that touches a sizzling charcoal, you want to be thinking that the feeling is there, even if in reality it happens in the somatosensory cortex and pain areas of the brain. The brain is full of such built-in, intentional illusions that are meant to improve our functioning, which is why we believe that the sound in the movie theater comes from the screen in front of us, even though the speakers are located on the side walls and behind us: functional mislocalizations.

William James, a pioneer of psychology, was one of the first to postulate that emotion actually arises from the body (the James-Lange theory). We feel anger or fear or elation in the body, and from this physical sensation the brain derives the cognitive representation of the corresponding emotion. According to this contentious theory, emotions do not start in the brain and then dictate the sensations to the body. Instead, the body responds directly to the perception of the stimulus—like the face of a lion or a smile from a loved one—and the change in the body is what gives the richness to the emotion in the brain. It does not mean that the body has a mind of its own, but rather the brain perceives the physical properties of the stimulus (colors, sounds, faces, smiles, and so on), this basic perception elicits the physical response in the body associated with it, and the ensued response in the body tells the brain what the emotion is. Emotion, according to this theory, is the brain's interpretation of the body's physiological reaction. We do not cry because we are sad; we are sad because we cry.

One more example, just because this theory is so counterintuitive. Let's say someone is yelling at you angrily. The physical features, such as the strength and frequency of his voice, the details of his facial expression, and his posture, are all perceived in the brain and swiftly conveyed to the body. The body responds to those specific physical features as it knows associatively. Then your brain figures, if my body recoils, my heartbeat goes up, and sweat develops on my skin, I must be frightened. Now also the brain knows the emotion. This may seem a bit circular and cumbersome, but it still shows that the most prominent figures, including the father of modern psychology and many after him, see the body as a major source in how we feel.

The body's emotional expressions play another important role. The emotional expression on our body, which of course includes the face, is meant to communicate to others how we feel. Just like we can infer a dog's mood from its tail, we can infer a much richer repertoire of emotions from the entire expressive bodies of our fellow humans. We are not necessarily conscious of how much we convey with or perceive from expressive faces and bodies, from surprise to fear, from alertness to thrill, and from boredom to disgust. In fact, it is not clear that the verbal language we use to describe our emotions has much of an effect on our companion, who has access to everything the body gives away.

Types of Thought

The frequency of different words in our environment has always interested people, because such measures reflect what is "trending" and what is currently on the public's mind, simply counting the words that appear most frequently in newspapers, books, radio, TV, and the Internet. The word "think" has been in the top 100 since the beginning of those accountings. John Dewey in his book *How We Think* says it is the most frequent word (which he might have meant figuratively), and in my recent check it was number 75. But any way we look at it, people talk about thinking and thoughts often. This should not come as a surprise, given that thinking is a most central activity of our life.

We tend to think about our thinking as a single monolithic process. Subjectively, it seems that our thoughts come and go, sometimes they stay a little longer, but basically it is the same train of thought with only the topics changing. But thoughts can be surrounding the same topic for a long time or jump associatively from one thought to another; they can be narrow or broad in the scope of the semantic ground that they cover; they can go fast or slow; they can be intended thoughts or intrusive thoughts; they can be generated from within or triggered by a stimulus in our environment; and they can be words, images, or sounds.

There are different thought patterns and many more than one type of thinking. By type, or pattern, of thinking, it is meant here the process of thinking proper, not the content of thought. It is how the car drives, not who is inside that car. We can be thinking about watermelons, skydiving, root canal, or death, but, regardless, we can be thinking about those topics in various manners that differ in nature. Those different types of thinking patterns are determined by our state, such as mood and context, and can help (or hurt) in achieving different goals. Here is a survey of the main types of thought.

Associative Thinking

Thoughts are composed of concepts. As described earlier, our memory of experience and knowledge can be seen as a giant web of nodes, where each node is a concept. Thinking of any concept is like visiting that node and activating what is represented by that node. It can be the color "red," the word "nice," the feeling "warmth," the face of "grandma," or the taste of "halva." Thinking patterns differ in how they advance on this web. Associative thinking specifically means that thought advances consistently from one concept to another concept that is associated with it. For example, you think about an apple, which makes you think about Isaac Newton, which makes you think about gravity, which makes you think about physics, which makes you think of your school days, which makes you think about your first crush, which makes you think about love, which makes you think about your kids, which makes you think about your age, which makes you think about working out, and so on. It progresses seamlessly, based on your own specific web of nodes and connections.

Those associations in our brain are a result of our experience with the world. Associations between related objects (chair–table, nurse–doctor) are called statistical regularities because statistically they tend to occur regularly together in our world. We accumulate such regularities of co-occurrences with experience and store them in memory as associations. The more frequently two concepts happen together in our world, the stronger they are connected in the brain. Compare a frequent pair like fork–knife with the less frequent pair fork–napkin and with the even less frequent pair fork–soup. In this example, the node "fork" will be connected with "knife," "napkin," and "soup," but with different strengths and thus later also with a different likelihood of being activated together.

Grouping items in our brain in an associative manner confers a large benefit both for a more economical storage in memory as well as for a more efficient retrieval of information back from memory. It is easier to store new things together with older things related to them that are already in memory, like representing scuba tanks together with the memory representation of a diver and other scuba equipment. Such associative storage naturally makes it easy to find and retrieve things from memory when you need them. Associative activations also serve as the basis for predictions in the brain. That a sound of a train is linked in our brains with a sight of a train or that a fire is associated with high temperature helps you optimize your interaction with the environment based on your past experience.

Associative thinking can be fast or slow, even if in both cases the concepts expand by association. When it is fast, it is akin to manic thinking and can be exhilarating. Associative thinking is linked with different states and personality traits, predispositions, talents, and disorders. Highly associative thinking is tied with creativity, as manifested by extraordinary insights and original problem solving, for example. Individuals with attention deficit hyperactivity disorder (ADHD) are highly associative and tend to be more creative (but less so when medicated).[6] When people are overly associative, seeing links when they are considered just loose associations for the rest of us, or where there are none, they may be diagnosed with delusions and psychiatric disorders such as schizophrenia. On the other extreme, when thinking is cyclical and ruminative around a certain topic for long durations, individuals may show signs of anxiety or other mood disorders such as depression.

Ruminative Thinking

Ruminative thinking is a recurrent pattern that tends to surround the same topic, circling it over and over again. A ruminative mind would dwell on the same incident or episode, examine it from multiple angles, repeatedly, irrationally, while typically agonizing over it. You think about a missed opportunity from yesterday, what it means, the loss, your image in the eyes of others, you could have become so rich, why did you have to get cold feet at the last minute, you were never good at taking risks, you will never get anywhere, and all over again. A less ruminative you, however, would think about it, perhaps learn a lesson, and move on.

Being stuck on the same topic is not synonymous with being intensely focused. When we are focused, the mental scope of what occupies our mind is indeed also narrow in terms of the conceptual volume it encompasses, but there is progress. When solving a complex math problem, or when designing a tree house, you are focused on the details, but there is a start and an end to the process. In rumination, you just go in circles.

We all ruminate from time to time, but sustained periods of rumination can have pathological outcomes. For example, ruminating about an expected future event ("I am not really prepared for my talk, my slides look awful, what if the air conditioner will not work and I will start showing sweat stains, so embarrassing, they are not going to like me") is akin to being anxious. It is normal. But when anxiety becomes an inherent, chronic pattern of the individual, constantly worrying and ruminating about what will happen next, this can develop into clinical anxiety, which can be debilitating and require treatment. When constantly ruminating about the past, mood also deteriorates, and the individual in this case might develop clinical depression. Indeed, anxiety and depression usually go together, a comorbidity in professional jargon, which means that individuals afflicted by one typically also suffer from the other. What they have in common, and also with many other psychiatric disorders, is the ruminative nature of thought.

Obsessive Thinking

Obsessive thoughts are the hallmark of obsessive-compulsive disorder (OCD). They are recurrent, persistent, and typically negative, though not necessarily circular, as in rumination. The more you try to stop those obsessive thoughts, the more obsessive they become. One can display obsessive thoughts along with other disorders, such as post-traumatic stress disorder (PTSD), panic attacks, and phobias. But not all obsessive thoughts are associated with a disorder. They can be perfectly natural for all of us at certain times, like being obsessed with a debt you have or with the whereabouts of the beautiful target of your infatuation. Obsessive thoughts are usually unwanted and seem to never cease.

Intrusive Thoughts

Intrusive thoughts are not really a thinking type proper, but rather a thought phenomenon. They are thoughts that are not voluntary, not invited, and usually not desired because they are negative, intruding on our ongoing chain of thoughts with no apparent relevance. In contrast with obsessive thoughts, intrusive thoughts occur only intermittently, but their intrusion can nevertheless be major. These could be intrusions from memories of trauma, persistent fears, or worries. Such intrusions can be paralyzing and possibly involve a host of negative feelings and emotions associated with the intruding thought. That said, we can also experience spontaneous activations of good memories, like a nice comment or a fun vacation, that just pop up unannounced, which still constitutes an intrusion because it interjects an otherwise unrelated thought sequence. The intrusion can also be a solution for some problem that bothered us earlier, and now a solution emerges after some subconscious "incubation" period. Clearly, not all intrusive thoughts are bad.

Note that the concept of "thoughts" and the concept of "memories" are being used here and throughout the book almost interchangeably. They are not identical, but they are highly related. Thoughts consist of activated memories (but not only). Everything we know, everything we remember from experiences, everything we fear, everything we anticipate, all the words we know, and all the feelings we remember are stored in memory. When you think about what your neighbor said to you in the elevator last night, it is a thought that was created by reactivating a piece of memory that was stored and dormant until you called for it. You know the capital city of Italy, but it is dormant (not anymore . . .) until you retrieve it and make it part of your ongoing thoughts. Memories are like files on shelves, lying there, waiting to be activated internally by you, or by external events, "retrieval cues" as we call them, that you encounter, like watching a commercial with an actor you have seen before, in a movie, on your last date with Eden, which is connected with many memories that are now reactivated in a chain reaction. An activated memory is a thought or part of a thought. But not all thoughts originate from memory. Consider simulations, those mental "dress rehearsals" we do so often. You pull some ingredients from memory, like how people are usually dressed at the beach, how exotic beaches tend to look, and the image of someone you would like to be with, and you construct a simulation of an experience that has not happened, at least not yet, with that person, on an exotic beach. Your thought now is partly novel and partly old from memory.

Curious Thought Disorders

In my mind, psychiatry is one of the best occupations one could dream of. Not only that you get to help people, but you get to watch the human mind in its full splendor. This is sometimes called neurodiversity to highlight the fact that variation from norm is not necessarily a disorder or a disease, but rather a manifestation of the healthy differences that make us interesting individuals and a thriving society. In psychiatry you get to tap the human mind and what might be the human soul closer than any other human. Observing thought patterns that have gone awry is magnificent and scary at the same time. We are so attached to our own worldview, and subjectively so convinced that the inner world of our fellow humans is similar to ours, that seeing someone talking to the air, being sure he is the son of God, or talking incoherently nonstop always feels at first like you are watching someone acting. Considering thought disorders provides a window like no other.

The first is *derailment*, sometimes referred to as loosening of associations. Although typically considered in clinical contexts, derailment is not always a disorder. As the name implies, derailment means getting off topic (either in thought or in talking). The individual drifts with the stream of ideas, never to return to the starting point. The discourse of ideas is not necessarily coherent and related. It is also often accompanied by intense emotions, like in rapid manic thinking. Derailment is seen in patients with schizophrenia, who tend to be highly and loosely associative (meaning that they see strong associations where for others the association is remote or loose).

A good everyday life metaphor for this condition is people who drink alcohol or smoke drugs that attenuate their inhibition and leave them with streaming ideas and a subjective sense of exceptional creativity (only to wake up the morning after and realize that what seemed like a great discovery last night is not that great in the morning . . .). Nevertheless, derailment thinking is sometimes conducive of creativity, possibly via what is called *lateral thinking*, which is characterized by flow that is not linear and where the logic applied when thinking about a problem is less apparent. Derailment thinking is sometimes also called *tangential* thinking, wandering with no return. Using "tangential," "lateral thinking," and "derailment" to refer to a similar pattern of thinking can be really confusing. I bring it up here to make the point that terminology should not be taken too seriously. (They say a scientist would rather use his colleague's toothbrush than his terminology . . .) Regardless of names, these various phenomena illustrate the many ways thought can progress, in order and in disorder. And there are more such demonstrations, most of which emphasize the tight link between memory and thinking and between thinking and speaking.

The next interesting thought disorder is *circumstantiality*, which refers to thoughts and speech that go around the idea in circles, with too many unnecessary details (we all have friends like this). Circumstantiality is different from derailment in that the individual eventually gets to the point. Another one, *poverty of speech*, is just the opposite, where the content of thought and consequently the speech are severely impoverished and less informative.

There is still a long list of curious phenomena that clinicians observe in patients and that reflect on our understanding of the thinking process, including blocking, where the train of thought can be suddenly blocked; flight of ideas, where ideas leap abruptly yet still somewhat coherently; a flow of incoherent words that are not related to each other; an obsessive reference of everything back to the self; and more. An odd disorder that also has to do with associations is *clang associations*, where thought and speech progress in rhymes rather than by meaning. This is usually present in patients with psychosis and in bipolar disorder.

As in many avenues of neuroscience, disorders are not just a clinical issue, but they also challenge us a great deal about our understanding of the operation of the brain in its normative, or neurotypical, form. For example, how is it possible for a thought to be blocked abruptly? Whatever happened to the train? What determines the speed of thought, and what determines the breadth of the associations covered?

Perhaps the best-known and the most telling thought disorders are *delusions* and *hallucinations*. Delusion is a distortion of reality, interpreting the world profoundly incorrectly, which predominantly includes paranoia and delusion of grandeur. Interestingly, psychotic patients that exhibit delusional thoughts hold them in exceptional conviction. Indeed, confidence in those distorted beliefs is part of the criteria for diagnosing delusions.

Pause for a second to appreciate the amazing complexity of our mind. A brain, which might look just like yours or mine, strongly believes that he is being followed or that it belongs to Napoleon, and no counterevidence can change its mind. A brain is made up of tens of billions of neurons, each of which functions like a switch, each connected to many other neurons. On top of the immensity of this web, there are many neurotransmitters and other molecular mechanisms in the mix. Where do you find Napoleon in there? We are pretty far from being able to explain such strong and distorted beliefs.

Hallucination, to be distinguished from delusions, is a perception of something that is not there, something that is made up, imagination that is mistaken for reality. They can be highly vivid and occupy a very specific location in space, and they can appear as visual, auditory, and in other modalities. While hallucinations are common in various psychiatric disorders, they can also occur with certain drugs or while falling asleep, waking up, or being deprived of sleep.

Our mind is often busy with mental simulations of what-if scenarios. Imagine if you thought that those mental simulations are actually happening, that you are actually flying, making love with that model, or drowning in the ocean. Similarly, think about imagery, our ability to bring up an image and see it in our mind's eye very vividly, perhaps also manipulate it, like mentally rotating Tetris cubes. We know simulations and imagery are inside our brain, and we usually do not confuse what is happening inside and what is happening outside.

In and Out

Our thoughts can be generated by an external stimulus, such as a sentence we overhear on the train, the smell of a pie as we enter home, or the brushing of your cat on your leg. They can also be triggered internally, as when you plan on inviting your sister and her new boyfriend for lunch and you start wondering if her boyfriend, whom you have met only once before, is genuinely nice or if it was just a show. But most of the time, the source of the thought is not exclusively internal or external. It is often a combination, and in addition we keep going back and forth between our internal and external worlds.

Fanaticizing, for example, that you, and not Tom Brady, are the quarterback in the Super Bowl is also a thought, and you know it is a thought. You know it is happening inside your head. But this is not something we are born with; it is a skill and knowledge we acquire as we grow up. For babies, distinguishing inner from outer events is not so easy or even present. An infant is initially less able to distinguish the physical from the mental world, what is an object and what is a thought. Mindwandering starts in earnest a bit later.

CHAPTER THREE

THE JOURNEY FROM NOW

I STILL REMEMBER VIVIDLY A STRIKING DEMONSTRATION I EXPERIENCED WHILE watching a James Bond movie several years ago. I like to sit in the front seats in theaters so that I can immerse myself in the movie. At some point, the bad guys were chasing 007 on speedy snowmobiles, an intense chase, occupying my entire visual field with bright colors and fast motion, while an engulfing sound system was tearing my eardrums apart. But my mind has a mind of its own, and it decided to wander (the act of mindwandering is known for being a nonconscious process). My thoughts carried me away so far and so deep that the next thing I knew, a satisfied Bond was sipping his martini at the bar in an ice palace; I apparently missed that entire chase. (I later checked: it was a four-minute chase.) Our mindwandering forces can be so powerful as to overrun the actual input coming from our senses. Bright sights, loud sounds, and our entire situational awareness can be missed and not registered because of more powerful thoughts. External physical reality can be overwritten by internal mental processes. That is amazing, and hard for a brain scientist to accept.

The brain, fantastic as it is, still has limited capacities: limited memory, limited attention, limited computational power, and so on. Just like the central processing unit of a computer (a terrible analogy for the brain, except in this context . . .) has to divide its capacity between multiple competing processes—the user's commands, background communication, requests from peripheral units such as the mouse or a printer—the brain has to divide what it has to offer between the processes that demand some resources. The brain, too, prioritizes which process gets what, and whatever it allocates comes out of the 100 percent it has, which ultimately diminishes the capacities left for other processes. For example, you could compute 16 x 93 in your head more easily and successfully if you are not distracted by other demands such as loud music or a conversation nearby that competes over the same resources that you need for that computation. It is a zero-sum game. So, if we wander, we perceive less, and if we are drawn into a certain experience, we wander less.

While the James Bond story is obviously an extreme and informal example, it is clear that we need our full mind for a full experience. What may be less clear is how much we miss about our lives when our mind is being hijacked by our thoughts, which apparently can be just as intense as reality. Like Rabbi Nachman of Breslev said, "You are wherever your thoughts are. Make sure your thoughts are where you want to be."

Developed to Wander

Our proclivity for mindwandering and daydreaming leans heavily on the prefrontal cortex, which resides in the very front of the brain. It matures later in life, in our early to midtwenties, which is considerably later than it takes for the rest of the brain to develop, and it takes it so long to mature for a good reason. The prefrontal cortex can be seen as the chief executive officer of the human brain (and indeed is often thought to be what separates us from all other animals). It is central for executive functions such as decision making, behavioral control (like avoiding impulsive behavior),[1] the evaluation of reward, understanding consequences, planning, what-if simulations, and other high-level cognitive processes. All these require knowledge that is hard earned through experience. For example, how would you know what to pack for a trip, what you can and cannot say to a stranger you are standing next to in line, or how to anticipate your friend's reaction to a surprise visit without relying on past occurrences of such or similar situations? The more experience you have, the more knowledge you have accumulated and the more prepared you are for an increasing number of circumstances.

This evolving body of experience-based knowledge is also the basis for the processes going on in our mind when we wander. Imagining yourself on a hammock tied between two coconut trees, simulating how you would feel if you were bitten by a dog on your thigh, or figuring out the intentions of your colleague when he said that you are a genius all require a reference to what you already know. Mindwandering relies on what we have stored in memory, which is why young children wander to a lesser extent.

Over the next several years, starting at about age five, children's brains begin consolidating more and more memories, and they head off on their departure from the now. Of course, this is hardly a pure tragedy. Developing a good memory is crucial in life, not the least of which is memory's role in the emergence of our sense of self. It's fair to say that, in many respects, our memory *is* who we are. Our sense of self is largely composed of our memories of our experiences, our preferences, our fears, our desires, our hopes and disappointments, and the beliefs we have formed. As we consolidate more memories, our minds increasingly engage in wandering, heading back into the past and pondering the future. By about ages nine to eleven, kids' minds are generally wandering about 20 to 25 percent of the time.[2]

Until not too long ago, mindwandering was taken as a nondesired drift that disrupts our mind, mood, and behavior. One prominent exception is the work of Jerome Singer, the pioneer of the study of daydreaming and of advocating daydreaming as a constructive mental tool.[3] Of course, some daydreaming might include negative, sometimes obsessive content and present an obstacle for our attempts to accomplish a certain goal. Indeed, left to their own devices, people seem to gravitate toward the negative quite often.[4] But other such reveries are welcome, playful, creative daydreams that should be nourished, as was later also promoted by Jonathan Schooler and colleagues.[5] Spending time with the younger generations, I learned about the appeal of watching movies and online videos on higher speed, at one and a half times the original speed or even faster. This option is now incorporated in various applications, so I can listen to a lengthy recorded message from a bored aunt quicker. This clearly saves time, but it also robs us of opportunities for creative mindwandering, as well as of memory consolidation, which also requires pauses in stimulation.

The vast majority of research on mindwandering has been directed toward trying to figure out its content. What is it that we think about when there is no task at hand that demands all our mental resources? We will get to the specifics of this productive and fascinating research in the next three chapters. But before that, I will describe the link between mindwandering and the cortical infrastructure that serves it.

The DMN Is Where Mindwandering Takes Place

Cognitive neuroscience is a meeting of two worlds: cognitive psychology and neuroscience, with different means and approaches, different terminologies, and radically different levels of explanation (abstract thinking and decision making in one end, neurotransmitters and synapses in the other, for instance) that need to be welded properly. As a cognitive neuroscientist, my scientific allegiance is to both ends of this explanatory spectrum. Here, the cognitive psychologist part makes me eager to understand the high-level concept of mindwandering, its content and its function, while my neuroscientist part does not even know what a mind is and aims to understand things in the most concrete and mechanistic level. We are far from understanding the basic neural elements of mindwandering—we cannot yet explain what a thought is—but looking at those central issues with both approaches simultaneously and alternately is the surest way to make both worlds meet and advance.

Part of the thinking practiced in scientific research might seem strange or unnecessary for someone looking from the outside, and the evolution of research surrounding mindwandering and the DMN provides one excellent example. On the one hand, we all accepted the intriguing existence of an ever-active default mode network in the brain. On the other, we know firsthand that our mind wanders regularly and frequently, especially when nothing else is happening. Yet this is not sufficient for one to argue that the DMN is the cortical platform that carries mindwandering in the brain. At times of no task and no goal we can only wander, and the only brain regions that are active during such times of idleness are in the DMN, but this intuitive link still had to be demonstrated clearly and unequivocally before we can make this claim with confidence. And just to show how not straightforward this link was at the time, this demonstration was groundbreaking enough to be published in one of the most prestigious journals, *Science*.[6] In that seminal work, Malia Mason, afterward a postdoc in my lab, scanned participants' brains with fMRI and had them mindwander so that she could look for a possible correlation between the extent of mindwandering and activity in the DMN.

Looking into someone's mind is far from a trivial task. In fact, it is hard for one to even observe his own mind. Distortions, lack of mental skills, and emotional interference, to name a few, obscure our mind from us and more so the minds of others. Functional MRI or any other brain-imaging technique can see brain structure and brain activity, but there is still a long way to being able to infer the actual mind. Imagine a crumbled notebook paper as a metaphor. Structural MRI and other anatomical measures would tell us the geometry and topography of that paper. Functional MRI and other electrophysiological measurements would tell us what letters are where. But putting this all together to understand the meaning of the text on that paper would still be unattained. Similarly, while we have advanced and are now able to map tiny brain tissues, neuronal activity, and cortical connectivity, we do not understand how together they give rise to our magnificent yet elusive mind.

Until we can peek into the mind directly, psychologists have devised indirect methods that are used as reasonable approximations for what is happening in our test subjects' minds. One of them is *thought sampling*, in its different flavors. In thought sampling, we usually stop our subjects (participants) at random points during a task and ask them about their thoughts: the content ("Have you been thinking about white bears?"), its relevance ("Is what you are thinking right now directly relevant for your current task?"), and so on. Of course, this method, too, has limitations. For example, subjective reports are, well, subjective and thus prone to distortions. Furthermore, a participant would tend to want to appease the experimenter or to appear in a certain way, which may also contaminate her responses. Such limitations are largely mitigated by proper instructions, by creating a specific atmosphere in the experiment, and by sampling a large-enough group of individuals.

Using such thought-sampling methods and looking particularly at intervals when subjects' minds had wandered off, Mason et al. were able to find a direct correlation between the extent of wandering and the extent of DMN activation. Mission accomplished. They further concluded that wandering is a baseline of our mind, interrupted only for tasks and goals. Now we know that when we do not do anything that requires our directed attention, we wander, and when we wander, we do it on the cortical network that is the DMN. This was a great step forward because it opened up the way, and the race, for understanding what it is that occupies our minds for such long stretches of our waking hours.

"Mindwandering" is a broad term. The main processes that are believed to make up the content of mindwandering are thoughts about the self, thoughts about others, predicting, planning and simulating possible futures, and more. In the next three chapters, we will go deeper into the main processes with which the DMN has been implicated.

CHAPTER FOUR

WHAT DO WE WANDER ABOUT? OUR SELF FIRST

I MAGINE SOMEONE WITH WHOM YOU HAVE THE LONGEST POSSIBLE RELA-tionship. It is intense and it is continuous; it is deep and intimate. You are warm to each other, but you are also very critical of each other. You tell your darkest secrets to that someone, but you also cheat and delude them. You know what's good for them, but you often do the exact oppo-site, while making up sophisticated and convincing excuses to appease them. You can be awfully proud of that someone, but the next day you want to run away from them. In return, that someone talks nonstop. They hamper your interaction with others and the quality of your ex-perience of the world. That someone keeps wanting to be at the center of your interest, but also make you feel guilty with disapproval. Love and hate, construction and destruction, genuine and false: seems like an impossible relationship; could someone like that exist? Yes, this someone is you. Our relationship with our *self* is the richest, most loving, most intricate, most meaningful, but also the least rational relationship we can have. And it is a relationship we do not fully understand. In his text *Tao Te Ching*, Lao Tzu says, "Knowing others is wisdom. Knowing the self is enlightenment."

When I Am Critical of Myself, Who Is Critical of Whom?

The self is a slippery mental construct that defies a clear and consensual definition. Indeed, I still remember how odd it sounded to me when I first learned that people study the self. What do we mean by "self"? The great psychologist and philosopher William James distinguished between two types of self, *I* and *Me*, which represent two different mental perspectives. Intuitively, in one perspective (I) the self is an agent, thinking, judging, and acting, and in the other perspective (Me) the self is an object. The self as object includes both physical (body) and abstract (our beliefs) properties, and the self as an agent is an observer and evaluator. Importantly, Me is experiencing and I is reflecting. Wittgenstein, as always, has said it most economically: I as an object and I as a subject.

It seems philosophers have been pondering the self since the beginning of time: Descartes, Locke, Hume, Tao Te Ching, Plato, Aristotle, to name a few of the giants who dealt with this issue. And it is no wonder so many have, given how central the concept of self is for our ability to understand our being. Views, naturally, vary and include anything from spiritual views involving the soul to more materialistic views, and also vary anywhere between endorsing it to dismissing the existence of self. David Hume, for example, suggests considering the self as a commonwealth, a bundle of attributes that make up our self, although they are each constantly changing. The story of the ship of *Theseus* is a good metaphor for this way of thinking about the constant yet changing self:

> The ship wherein Theseus and the youth of Athens returned from Crete had thirty oars, and was preserved by the Athenians down even to the time of Demetrius Phalereus, for they took away the old planks as they decayed, putting in new and stronger timber in their places, insomuch that this ship became a standing example among the philosophers, for the logical question of things that grow; one side holding that the ship remained the same, and the other contending that it was not the same.[1]

When we look at the mirror, we see our self, same as the self we saw also ten years ago.

Perhaps not as in contrast as it may seem at first, one of the modern philosophers to address the issue of the self, Daniel Dennett, has famously equated the self to the concept of the center of gravity: a "convenient fiction" that does not exist but helps us solve problems. He compares the self to the center of gravity of a hoop, which is a point of nothingness in the air but still the center of gravity. Sometimes a good example is all we need. The topic of self connects with other central issues that interest philosophers and cognitive neuroscientists alike, such as the sense of agency and free will.

In spiritual, meditative philosophies, Buddhism chief among them, the idea of a permanent self is taken as an illusion. They argue that there is no individual existence that is separated from the rest of the world. In fact, Buddhism lists "the three marks of existence" as anattā (Pali for "nonself" or "nonsoul"), duḥkha (suffering), and aniccā (impermanence). If it sounds to you that Buddhism gives a pretty glum view about life, you are not alone. But this is a distorted first impression. Once

I dug deeper, both in studying and in practicing, I learned how liberating accepting nonself (or at least a diminished self), inherent suffering of some aspects in life, and that things do not exist permanently could be. I do not know that I will ever be able to completely accept nonself or suffering in my everyday life, but I found impermanence a most powerful idea to implement in my world. Last year, when visiting the breathtaking North of India with Noa, we saw monks diligently building a giant, intricate mandala out of fine and colorful sand, only to blow on it when it was completed and start a new one all over again, elaborate means for not forgetting impermanence and for not clinging. I tried to explain this to Nili, who was disappointed that we have not kept all her arts-and-crafts creations from kindergarten.

The idea of Buddhist practices is to dissolve the self, or the ego, as it is sometimes called (not a direct equivalent to what Freud dubbed ego, though). Dissolving the self through silent sittings is a major challenge, at least it was and still is for me, but we focus on the idea. To help us rid ourselves of our inherent attachment to our self, meditation teaches us to see the world as it is, rather than as our beliefs tell us. Of course, the rich and ancient Buddhist texts are much deeper and broader than the minimal description here. There are many scholars one can read; my own personal favorites at the moment are Alan Watts and Jiddu Krishnamurti.

Dissolving the self, or, in its more dramatic name, ego death, can reportedly also be achieved through the use of psychedelic drugs such as psilocybin, LSD, and DMT. Scientifically rigorous research on the effect of such psychedelics as well as on the Buddhist methods for dissolving the self has started only in recent years. Nevertheless, the consistent reports from many individuals that the effect that their mind ceases to differentiate their self from the rest of the world are intriguing. I find it fascinating that our mind can hold such radically different views about the self and that we might be able, at least in theory, to switch between self and no self in certain conditions. Furthermore, ego dissolution might potentially carry a significant therapeutic value for certain conditions such as depression and PTSD. In later chapters we will see that we do not need to go very far to experience some loss of self: when we are totally immersed in an endeavor that is really engaging, or extremely threatening, we also cease to experience the self, during which the activity of the DMN is tamped down.

In psychology the self is taken to represent our identity, which includes cognitive, emotional, social, and other aspects of what makes us who we are. It is also believed to be composed of subselves, such as self-awareness, self-knowledge, self-esteem, and more. Naturally, the self relies heavily, if not exclusively, on memory: remembering the aspects of who we are, what we like and do not like, what we fear and what we desire, our connections with the world, our identity in our own eyes and in the eyes of others, and so on.

In clinical psychology there is another interesting discussion about a variant of the self. Pioneered by the great psychoanalyst and thinker Donald W. Winnicott, it is said that we have a true and a false self to deal with. (Erich Fromm later called these original self and pseudo self.) According to Winnicott, the true self is the sense we develop as infants of our experience in the world, of reality, and of our spontaneous and authentic responses to our surroundings. Maintaining and growing that true self requires the proper responses from our caregivers, primarily our parents. When our actions are not receiving the desired response, we, as infants, start to cater to their expectations instead. This leads to developing a pleasing false self that makes us less authentic, less spontaneous, and more adhering to the expectations of our surroundings. We lose ourselves. This distinction between true and false selves is not synonymous with the Me and I of James, but it does bolster our intuition that the construct of self, illusory or not, is central to our sense of being.

Cognitive philosophers often divide the self into two types. One is *the narrative self*: the conceptual individual identity that persists over time, the self we tell our narrative about, which is parallel to the *I*; it is the reflector, the agent, self. The second is *the minimal self*: a momentary self, which is akin to the *Me*, the object that experiences. These two types of self have both been linked to our psychological well-being, and they each seem to be mediated by somewhat different brain regions and networks.

The brain behind the self is being gradually studied more extensively, but we already have ample evidence that the DMN is the cortical network most tightly mediating our sense of self and that the content of mindwandering involves self-referential processes. This has been demonstrated by experimental manipulations in the lab. Let's take one such study as an example, an fMRI study that aimed to test directly for a connection between self-related processes and the DMN.[2] There were three experimental conditions in this study. In the self-referential condition, participants watched names of traits, such as "lucky" or "skeptical," and had to report whether this word described them. This forced them to think about themselves. In the non-self-referential condition, participants had to report the number of vowels in each word presented to them. Although the words presented are similar in both conditions, counting vowels is much less personal and thus much less about the self compared with relating traits to yourself. The third condition was a "resting-state" condition, which is when we tell participants to rest and not do anything and when mindwandering and the DMN are typically being mapped for individuals. The authors reported a significant overlap between the activation elicited in the DMN by the self-referential condition and the activation elicited by the resting-state, mindwandering condition, much more than in the non-self-referential (counting vowels) condition. Such studies provide support for our evolving revelation of the link between the DMN and the sense of self.

More specifically, the DMN has been implicated with the narrative self or self-related processing. The minimal self, the one that experiences "firsthand," also engages regions such as the insula and the temporoparietal junction responsible for multisensory integration and interoception, which makes sense, given that the experiencing involves integration of information arriving from multiple senses.[3] Furthermore, research such as that conducted by Aviva Berkovich-Ohana demonstrates that DMN activity is reduced with the diminishing sense of self through meditation.[4]

Much work is yet to be done in understanding the neuroscience of the self. This is a highly complex area of study, but the link between mindwandering and this vital brain function is well established. We are probably all familiar with how obsessive, and upsetting, our mind's preoccupation with self-reflection can be, and this is one reason that gaining some power over our mindwandering can be so life enhancing.

Self-Chatter

We talk to ourselves all the time. The self is at the basis, even the cause, of our self-talk, inner speech, inner narrator, and inner critic, that internal voice that can torment us. This has been established through empirical and theoretical work by researchers such as Ethan Kross of the University of Michigan, Charles Fernyhough of Durham University in England, and Michael Gazzaniga of the University of California, Santa Barbara.[5]

We can look at inner speech as a habit of the mind, but it is more like a trait. The inner speech could roughly be divided into an inner dialogue and an inner monologue (and there are other names, including verbal thinking, covert self-speaking, and more). In the inner *monologue*, we talk to ourselves: we narrate our experience (bad), rehearse upcoming conversations we plan or imagine we are going to have, as well as replay and redress past verbal interactions we had with others. There is relatively little research into inner speech, surprisingly little given how often we engage in it, but it is understandable because it is a hard phenomenon to study for technical reasons. We cannot really peek into someone's head to examine their inner speech, which is a most personal experience, and individual self-reports from participants in experiments cannot get a scientific study very far. The two main dominant theories about the function of inner speech concern the development and control of cognition and behavior, and the other has to do with working memory.[6] But another role for the inner speech is translating abstract thoughts and feelings into words and in a communicable manner.

We can accomplish a great deal without words, from flying a kite to making love. The reason we are so linguistic is because just as words are the primary way with which we can convey our thoughts to others, it is also the main way for us to communicate with ourselves about our lives. The language used in our conscious mind is our spoken language; imagine how we would understand our thoughts if it were not. Language is as much a tool, or an interface, for communication as it is a tool for thought. The fact that we speak to ourselves in grammatically correct, complete, and coherent sentences just goes to show it is a facade. This could help understand how preverbal children and possibly animals could still be thinking even without having developed language capabilities. The thinking part is in place to some degree, but the communication of these thoughts, which is made possible with language, is lagging.

Our inner speech is akin to thinking aloud. All words are thoughts, but not all thoughts are words. There are visual images, music, bodily sensations, emotions, and other nameless feelings. Beyond the possible functions of speaking to ourselves to promote development, memory, mental health, cognition, behavior, simulations, and planning, we use inner speech to fabricate, to ourselves more than to others, the motivations for our thoughts, desires, and actions. Furthermore, inner speech is also an efficient tool for translating information arriving to us from the subconscious into a language that our conscious mind can later communicate. As much as scientists have dared to approach the subconscious mind with rigorous experiments (not an easy career direction, which is why not enough has taken place yet), we do not know what language is spoken in subconscious land. But when a thought is mature enough to cross the border and present itself consciously, like revelations in psychoanalysis or when insights strike, it has to be presented in a language we can understand. Sometimes even this is still not enough, and we are left with incomplete sentiments such as "I don't know why, but I just can't stand this guy" or "This deal smells fishy, I am out." Most of the arguments remain behind the scenes and cannot be uttered even internally because of lack of access. To tell myself in actual words inside my head "I will go for a run around five o'clock" means to make myself aware of this plan I have just made. It could be a plan that I devised consciously or a plan that was decided for me subconsciously, but it is not before it is spoken in plain words that I am aware of my plan. Thus, inner speech can also be seen as the language of consciousness.

The inner *dialogue* offers additional functions to those offered by the inner monologue. Inner dialogue is like playing chess with yourself: you are not fooling or tricking anyone; there are no surprises; things are predictable. That said, this is our main method of addressing the elusive self, a conversation between Me and I. It is Me trying to appease my inner critic, a conversation about right and wrong, good or bad, and the eternal search for approval.

I: We need to tell her it is not working between us.

ME: Yes, but then we will never see her again, and I loooove spending time with her.

I: Well, it is not fair to keep her hoping.

ME: Just a little more. Come on, she's a grown-up, and she can always leave.

I: No, this is not how we care for others; jeez, you are so selfish. Besides, being with her when you know it is wrong for both of you also keeps you from finding Ms. Right.

ME: Okay, but let's wait until after our vacation.

I: Sure, but do you think you can enjoy the vacation knowing that things are not for real? And will you stop procrastinating after that?

ME: Of course!

I: You mean like when you promised you would not procrastinate in that . . . ?

ME: Oh, remember that great idea I had about procrastination being good for creative incubation?

I: Diverting again. I give up. Enjoy your vacation, loser.

ME: You are coming with me, honcho, but please be quiet and let me immerse myself.

We negotiate moral and practical issues with that other inner someone, just like we negotiate with others. We can think of the two sides of an inner dialogue like a conversation between a teenager and her father; the teenager is experiencing, immersed, and generally wants to live in the moment, while the other self is the grown-up that judges and reflects. It is not a clear-cut or established distinction, but it is a good way for us to examine the typical agenda of the two voices in our heads.

This discussion of the self on its various flavors serves two purposes. First, it was presented here as one of the core contents occupying the default network and mindwandering. The next two chapters will discuss other such core contents. The second reason we want to be aware of the research and thinking about the self is to understand that our mind, and our experience, can vary dramatically depending on the perspective we take with our self. The general perspective we take in an experience can be either immersed or that of an outside observer, each of which leads to radically different qualities of experience. This distinction between observing and immersing bodes well with the distinctions done in the past and reviewed above, particularly with William James's Me versus I.

CHAPTER FIVE

THIS WAY SOMETHING POTENTIALLY WICKED COMES

THE SECOND POPULAR ACCOUNT OF WHAT IS OCCUPYING OUR MIND AND DMN when we wander is the process of figuring out others: their intentions, their dispositions, and their state of mind. And it is no wonder, with hindsight, that this heavy cortical machinery is working so intensely on understanding others. Getting a good read on what others are thinking and feeling is, to significantly understate the matter, perniciously tricky. Yet our survival is highly reliant on it. That's in part because getting a good sense of others helps perceive threats they may pose. But it's also vital in collaborating effectively with them. So, our minds evolved to engage hard at it. In fact, some evolutionary theorists suggest that the computational demands required for social interactions with others explain why we humans developed such large brains.[1]

Our Communication with Others and with Ourselves

Communication is critical for any interaction. Indeed, many human arguments stem from misunderstandings. This is not a scientific fact, but I am sure that it will resonate with many. After all, explaining what we mean is not the easy feat that it seems to be. Our subjective belief is that we are being understood and that our intentions, at least when they are honest, are perfectly clear. But there are many factors that stand in the way of information transfer.

Philosopher Ludwig Wittgenstein was fascinated with human communication and with the need for clarity. He saw the issue of explaining something to someone akin to transferring an image you have in your mind to that other person's mind in the most accurate manner. Our thinking is largely visual, so this is not a far-fetched metaphor. Assume you want to tell your friend from another planet that you love ice cream. Forget about explaining love for a moment and focus on the ice cream. How would you describe it? Cold, dairy, sweet, colorful, round on a cone, between solid and liquid? Would that be enough for your friend to understand what ice cream is, let alone its taste and the feelings that it evokes? Far from it. We usually do not encounter such discrepancies, and most people we talk to have been exposed to similar environments as we have, but the opportunities for misinterpretations are still vast. Take the example of someone saying "Yeah, right" or, better yet, "Forget about it," which is exceptional in its many meanings (watch the movie *Donnie Brasco* for a lengthy tutorial on this one). Detecting sarcasm requires extremely sophisticated semantic and social skills, which is why young children often fail to perceive it and why even the best AI-programmed personal assistants are dumbfounded by it. Try some sarcastic comments out with Siri or Alexa and see what you get. Another example for everyday obstacles in communication: asking permission to bring your dog to work. Your boss imagines a huge, scary, dirty, loud, and hyperactive bull terrier, while you meant to bring your depressed, sleepy white fur ball. Easy to see how different images in different minds can lead to misunderstandings between fellow humans.

We are not aware, at least not on an ongoing basis, of all the obstacles to clarity. In a regular conversation, we have expectations of what we are about to hear. We often anticipate the ending of our friend's sentence. We can be wrong, but nevertheless we tend to stick to our anticipation. What's more, our personal perception of reality is distorted in many ways, so in communication between two people it is two individual realities that are distorted in different ways trying to make sense of each other. And on top of that, we tend to understand words, concepts, ideas, feelings from our own standpoint. You imagine that this person's worldview is similar to yours. He says that what his drink tastes like is a lychee milkshake. He meant that it tastes bad because he hates lychee, but you think he loves his drink because you love lychee. And this is just an example of a benign misunderstanding due to lack of perspective taking, that concept we call Theory of Mind, the ability to get into somebody else's head. Indeed, our poor ability to imagine what is going on inside someone's mind, which typically stands in striking discrepancy with our confidence in our ability to do so, makes human communication a risky business.

But perhaps the biggest obstacle to our communication with others, as well as with ourselves, is our inability to access the origin of most of our own thoughts and feelings. We are simply not conscious of those sources, as elaborated earlier. By now, there are already fascinating and borderline scary findings on how much of our thoughts, emotions, choices, and behavior are determined behind the scenes of consciousness. The subconscious has multiple functions and benefits. (Let me qualify here that the term "subconscious" is highly controversial, both because there is no widely accepted definition for this concept and more so because many scientists do not even accept its existence. Addressing these controversies is beyond the scope here. Given that I will be avoiding some of Freud's main claims about the subconscious and focus more on mental processes of which we are simply not privy, the existing controversies are not that relevant.) The interesting benefits of subconscious operation include cognitive and affective functions. The cognitive include processes such as "incubation," whereby the subconscious continues to grind and try out multiple solutions to a problem until it reaches the best one and only then lets our conscious mind know about it. Indeed, mindwandering and the DMN are linked with *creative incubation*.[2] When this happens, the conscious self experiences it as a blazing insight, a gut response, a hunch, or an aha! moment of epiphany. That's how it feels. These behind-the-scenes processes can also be very boring, like continuing to try to recall the name of a certain person, so the subconscious rids our conscious mind of tedious details and frees us for more interesting mental endeavors. The other potential benefit of subconscious functioning is shielding us from overwhelming emotions and personal "issues" that are yet to be resolved when we are ready, but there is much less neuroscience research on that aspect.

The fact is that we are largely operated by our subconscious. Our control of our own life, in many domains, is an illusion. The subconscious makes a decision, and what is left for us to do is to use our conscious awareness (and creativity) to fabricate an excuse, our best guess, of why we do what we do. Mike Gazzaniga and Joseph LeDoux call it *the interpreter*, which is claimed to reside in the left hemisphere. It is as amusing as it is fascinating to see how our desire to feel in control of our mind drives us to make up an account for each thought and action, just not to leave any mental movement of ours without personal ownership, a sense of agency. Somewhat reminiscent of our need to label everything with a name, our persistence in imagining sources for our thoughts and feelings is tied to our desperate need for meaning and certainty in the world. For a large part, the subconscious drives us, and the conscious mind makes up explanations.

It is not meant that everything is decided for us, the conscious us, by our subconscious mind. Our conscious mind is certainly responsible for many aspects of our rational, behavioral, and deliberative life. And more than its role in carving our choices, the conscious mind has an executive role in controlling the extent to which we listen to the thoughts and decisions coming to us from the subconscious. It is the gatekeeper, at least when we are able to exert the proper inhibitions. Plato spoke about the charioteer riding two horses, one noble (the conscious mind) and one beastly (the subconscious). We are not animals acting on whatever urges and impulses arise, but we still act on many of them without understanding why, and the result is that we are not in control as much as we would like to be. Even with choices that seem completely conscious and cerebral, there is a subconscious component, small or large, that we cannot appreciate because, well, it is subconscious.

After living in the United States for many years (I moved from Israel for my PhD studies with Maria, my then girlfriend, in 1994), we started pondering moving back when the opportunity presented itself. I remember on one of those trips I made to check that possibility, I was waiting for my connecting flight and decided to open my laptop and make a list of pros and cons for such a move compared with the position and other offers I had in the United States, careerwise but more so for the family, schools, security, financial, and all possible criteria I could think of. Israel was far from coming up first on that list I made, but I closed my laptop and I remember telling myself, "Okay, we are moving to Israel." It was the opposite of what that chart suggested, not much of an effect of the conscious mind on the eventual outcome.

We do not know much about subconscious content and processes, in spite of many great ideas that have been voiced over many years and that mainly go to show how much the subconscious fascinates us. But we do know a great deal, relatively speaking, about the cognitive and perceptual differences between the conscious and unconscious mind. (I am using "unconscious" and "subconscious" interchangeably, though there is no consensus that they are equivalent or representing different concepts.) We know that the conscious mind works serially, or sequentially, one operation after another, whereas the unconscious is more parallel in how it processes information. Additionally, the conscious mind is limited in capacity, in that performance in a cognitive task is constrained by the number of elements and the extent of mental load, whereas the subconscious is less affected by capacity.

Our lack of access for much of what drives us is why it is so impossible for us to be in touch with ourselves, or explain ourselves to others, or explain others to ourselves. We do not have much of an idea about the roots of our very being. Nature must have had good reasons to build us as such, but the result is a life filled with misunderstandings.

Perhaps the answer is not to explain, but to let our subconscious do its job without feeling a need to fabricate a narrative. Meditation is one possible method to achieve such a state of not clinging to the feeling of agency over what we think and do. Quieting the noise means quitting conscious attempts at explanation. Donald Winnicott once said that those who do not trust their subconscious keep a diary. I, for one, trust it.

The other day I went to lunch with Olivia, a woman I met at a meditation retreat a year ago. We talked only briefly there (well, it is a silence retreat after all . . .), and the only interaction since was that she texted me twice so that we could meet for coffee, and I have not responded until now for some reason. Two nearly complete strangers, meeting for an hour to eat and chat, yet we felt close, like old friends. How is it possible?

There are many others I have known for much longer and still do not feel as close with them. One answer is that our dispositions affect our perception and thus our communication. Much of life is happening inside our brains. We can be enemies or old friends, depending only on what we have inside. And, as we touched upon here, our ability to fathom what is really going on inside our mind, and in the minds of others, is quite limited. This is why our thinking about others' minds is called a *Theory* of Mind; we don't really know. Yet we are constantly engaged in it, because the content of somebody else's mind affects their behavior, and anticipating that behavior is of supreme importance for us on the receiving end of that behavior.

Theory of Mind in the DMN

ToM, sometimes called also *mentalizing*—our continuous attempt at deriving others' intentions, emotions, and beliefs—is the second proposed core content of mindwandering and the DMN. Research tying the two is recent but booming. Let us look again at a representative study that was seminal in making this link.[3] The goal of that study was to look for a potential overlap between the fMRI activity measured when participants are explicitly engaged in ToM and the fMRI activity in the DMN during rest (mindwandering), so that the then-hypothesized connection could be tested directly. A significant overlap would imply that during mindwandering our DMN is engaged in ToM. The researchers actually did more than that. They set out to look more broadly at whether the DMN is indeed the network mediating ToM, self-referential processes, and prospection (more on prospection in the next chapter), all of which have been suggested to be core contents of mindwandering, which had not been fully established at that time yet. Participants saw pictures of everyday scenes, such as a family sitting around a table at a restaurant, and were required to do one of three things. In the "self" condition, they were asked to relate that scene to themselves by using guiding propositions such as "Remember a time when you went out with your family." This instruction makes participants refer to their personal, autobiographical memory to retrieve their own experience. In the "prospection" condition, they would respond to the instruction "Imagine a time you will go out with your family," which makes them imagine a future event of theirs. In the third condition, ToM, they would answer the question "Imagine what the father in the picture was thinking and feeling," which obviously makes them engage in inferring another mind. As a control condition for comparison, participants also viewed "scrambled," meaningless pictures and had to press a button on the keyboard to emulate the actions of the other conditions. All three experimental conditions—self, prospection, and ToM—activated the DMN, much more than the control condition, and the activation pattern of the three conditions overlapped significantly. Not only did this study show that the DMN is involved in our ongoing ToM efforts, but it also clumped it with self-referential and prospection processes.

The DMN isn't the sole player in our ToM ponderings. A number of other parts of the brain are involved, such as the amygdala—often referred to, far too simplistically, as the seat of emotion—and the insula, which has been associated with a host of functions, ranging from situational awareness and bodily processes to emotion as well as cognitive and even motor functioning.

The full story of the neuroscience isn't yet known, but what we do know about ToM skills has helped me see the connections between the other work on the DMN and my own. As I kept putting people in the magnet, I realized that in making visual associations, people are doing a form of prediction based on past experiences. We're not just receiving visual inputs;

we're pulling out of memory all sorts of clues to help us construct a sense of what we are seeing. And this associative action was focused in the DMN.

More generally, as I elaborated earlier, associations are an elegantly simple yet extremely powerful tool that the brain is using for memory encoding and retrieval, as well as for helping us anticipate what's ahead. When we learn a new piece of information, we store it in our memory by connecting (associating) it to items that we have already stored in the past and that are related to it in some way. It might be encoding the shape of a blob of coffee by connecting it to an elephant because it reminds you of an elephant and that's a way for you to remember it, or memorizing a string of digits by finding some pattern or similarity. We also encode things by associations based on relevance. A chair is associated with a table, a fork is associated with a knife, a red light is associated with "stop," and an angry person approaching is associated with "take cover." The brain picks up co-occurrences, those statistical regularities, because things that occur together tend to be relevant together. Encoding with associations makes it also easier to retrieve that information. Our memory is a massive web of associations, where everything is connected with everything else, with some degrees of separation, just like another massive web of associative connections, the Internet. But beyond memory encoding and retrieval, associations are the medium for how we use prior knowledge to help us prepare for our future. A sound of a train makes you anticipate a train crossing, a smile from a woman on the other side of the bar may make you approach (though watch the end of the movie *Swingers* for a funny exception), and before going to a museum you know how to dress, that you will need money, and that the visit will last about a couple of hours. Even the most mundane steps in our lives are driven by memory-based predictions. Associations in the DMN would mean predictions in the DMN and in mindwandering.

How else would our mind advance from one node in its gigantic web of memories to another if not by associations? So it was deeply interesting to me that other researchers were coming to understand that ToM skills are also a type of prediction, also drawing on memory. But unlike our ability to use associations to anticipate occurrences in the external world, they are not as accurate when it comes to predicting others' inner working. We tend to be quite confident in our ToM interpretations of others, but they are, in fact, very largely simulations. They're fabricated scenarios of what people might be thinking and feeling, and might therefore do, more than factual observations, and they're heavily biased by our own past experiences. We think, "She just flicked her hair and looked slightly askance because she's attracted to me" or "He heard me just fine and is ignoring me, just like my father did so often." Naturally, the more we know a person, the more reliable are such associations and predictions. I can anticipate pretty accurately what a facial expression on my significant other's or kids' faces means, or how would they respond to what I am about to say, with high likelihood. But projecting this knowledge to other people is not as trustable as we would like it to be.

Most of us, most of the time, do not realize how much we're in the dark when theorizing about others' intentions. Being a neuroscientist doesn't help with this. A couple of months ago I was visiting the United States and decided to make a stop in Cambridge, Massachusetts. The first meeting I had was a catch-up dinner with two good friends, Daniel Gilbert and Jonathan Schooler, who also happen to be two luminous psychologists who have both written about mindwandering. During dinner, Dan told me that the following week he was going to be awarded the prestigious William James Prize at the upcoming meeting of the Association for Psychological Sciences in Washington, DC. He added that his three best friends would be taking him for drinks to celebrate after the ceremony, and I thought that I perceived that he was testing whether

I felt like a close enough friend to suggest that I'd join them. I said I would, and he responded that they would love for me to come along. All good. But, wait, maybe not . . .

For the next couple of days, I found myself tormented, wondering if I had misread Dan. Did he really mean he'd like for me to come, or was he just being polite? Had I barged in on their BFF gathering? What if I wrote to say that I couldn't make it after all? Would I offend him? I decided not to risk being a pain and went ahead and sent a note that unfortunately I couldn't make it. Dan sent a warm reply, as usual, and I had no better sense of whether I'd misread the situation. If I want to know exactly what he had in mind, I will have to simply come out and ask him—a good practice for all of us when we feel it is important to be sure we understand someone. That's because our ToM conjectures are often off base, sometimes wildly so.

The fact that our ToM interpretations are scenarios that we construct rather than pure observations, and that our brains engage in this activity by default, is showcased by how often we try to anticipate the ending of a friend's sentence. Yet, even so, we're often wrong. Furthermore, it's hard to stop ourselves from making these guesses. An amusing demonstration of this compulsion is a study that showed it is more distracting, in terms of attention and subsequent memory, to sit next to someone who is having a conversation on their cell phone than next to two people talking in person.[4] With the call, because we hear only one side of the conversation, our minds run rampant with trying to fill in what the other person is saying.

One of the most harmful effects of this tendency to construct mental scenarios about others is our proclivity to form first impressions of them, very rapidly, and then to have much too much confidence in those initial judgments. Note that first impressions are not theories of mind proper but rather more a theory of personality, but they do guide the way we infer others and in that sense are in the same category of ToM. As I continued my research on the DMN's role in predictions, I began exploring ToM operations, and I was to find that first impressions of others can be formed in as little as thirty-nine thousandths of a second.[5] As for our devotion to them, the lab of Alex Todorov at Princeton has shown that judgments made on pictures of unfamiliar candidates for governor in a remote state were highly predictive of actual results from the elections.[6] While that may suggest that those first impressions were uncannily accurate, the better interpretation is that voters in the state also formed their judgments about who to vote for largely on the basis of snap impressions, despite the barrage of candidate advertisements and news coverage in an election.

So far we have considered two core contents for what is in our wandering mind: our self and the self of others. There are other proposals for additional subtypes of information and processes taking place in the DMN, but now we turn to the one that is the foundation for them all.

CHAPTER SIX

FUTURE MEMORIES: LEARNING FROM IMAGINED EXPERIENCES

I WAS INTRIGUED BY THE FINDINGS ABOUT THE ROLE OF THE DMN IN SELF, ToM, and more as they began to emerge, in part because my own work in evaluating what the DMN is up to was so far afield at first. Eventually, my first studies on visual associative processing led me to my own findings about the DMN's predictive penchant. I began by putting people in the magnet and asking them to recognize objects to see what parts of the brain were involved in the process. A key early finding was that people perceive objects differently depending upon the context they're seen in. In the initial study, my first ever, we used cutouts of the beautiful figures made by an artist named Haro Hodson, who was a cartoonist for the *Daily Mail* and the *Observer*, among other newspapers.[1] As can be seen on page 70, we have no problem completing missing elements, and

we can readily recognize the figures although the information provided is highly sparse. In our experiment, we cut and presented individual objects such that they could appear in their original setting, in a nontypical setting, or alone in isolation. Context, which includes the identity of the objects around as well as their relative position in space, directly affected participants' predictions of what individual, otherwise ambiguous, objects might be. For example, the smoking pipe in (b) could not be recognized as a pipe when presented alone, but placing the guy's hat in its proper original location relative to it made the pipe recognizable in an instant. Same about the buttons in (c) and the purse of the lady in (g): simply putting something related next to them, in the proper position, makes those collections of meaningless pixels meaningful. The way we interpret things in our environment depends not only on the features of the thing we try to interpret, but also on the environment in which it appears. Associations generate predictions, which together help us understand our world.

Associative Predictions in Mindwandering

It was from this growing research that I realized that when we're visualizing, we're thinking associatively. We found that doing so recruited a big chunk of cortex, a massive network of interconnected regions. And when I compared this network to the DMN, they were strikingly overlapping.[2]

This was initially quite puzzling, because the majority of the literature on the DMN at that point, from the heavy hitters of the field, concerned the work on the sense of self and Theory of Mind just covered. How on earth could I explain that the DMN is also involved in making associations and thinking associatively? As I contemplated this conundrum, I realized that both thinking about ourselves and thinking about others lean heavily on associations between bits of information that are linked in our memory based on repeated experience. In considering what kind of person we are in any given moment, for example, we will often recall things we have said and done in the past in situations similar to that in which we find ourselves.

Our minds meander all over as they're making connections. I can portray how our thoughts ramble by analogy to the progression of a conversation among friends having dinner at a restaurant. John may comment about the horrible traffic he ran into on the way there but how he didn't really mind because his new car has such a great stereo that he enjoyed the chance to crank up the volume and get in some quality listening time. The mention of loud music might prompt Alexandra to bring up her father's hearing loss from defiantly playing Grateful Dead songs at high volume in his bedroom when he was a teenager. That might in turn lead Jess to lighten things up by saying she wished restaurants would offer Cherry Garcia ice cream for dessert, which might spark Adam to say he'd love some ice cream for dessert, despite being on a new diet, launching into how nonfat diets are actually bad for you. John might then weigh in about how bogus so much media coverage is when it comes to our health, with everyone suddenly shutting up for a couple of minutes when the food arrives before a new associative thread ignites.

Associations are the vehicle of mental drift. We can argue whether our mindwandering is a selected trait of evolution or a "bug" that is the side effect of having an associative mind that keeps on moving, but, either way, the mindwandering that associations afford is a mixed blessing. Vital as making associations is to much of finding our way in the world, this often again pulls us out of being fully present in the now. Associations are like a gravitational, attracting force, not letting us stay in one mental place for long before our mind is tempted to make the next associative jump because it is so easy to follow. In fact, the best way to pause our automatic tendency to wander is to actively apply inhibition, which is not always possible and is costly in terms of energy and in its negative effect on mood.

Our minds positively love to seize on associations, and it was delving into why that led me to realize one reason is that associations are enormously helpful in allowing us to predict what to expect on a moment-to-moment basis. While some efforts at prediction are fundamentally ill-conceived, like trying to anticipate when the stock market will take a plunge or what team will win the big game, and others, such as we've seen with ToM predictions, can be deeply flawed, so many of our daily predictions are not only quite accurate but crucial to our functioning. If we're making predictions about the immediate and relevant future based on associations built through experience, such as about how our body will react to bingeing on chocolate, we're often spot-on.

MOST OF WHAT WE DO IN LIFE IS BASED ON SUCH EXPERIENCE-BASED PREDICTIONS. Indeed, a huge amount of our functioning relies on them. We are constantly constructing if-then scenarios in our mind, much of which are boringly mundane. If I wear my dress shoes out with this light snow falling, I will probably slip. If the cat jumps up on the sideboard, he might knock that vase over. These cogitations are rendered mundane only because we rely on them so frequently, automatically, and often unconsciously.

As I and others continued studying how our mindwandering is engaged in prediction, a particularly fascinating finding to me was how much of it is devoted to a particular kind of prediction: constructing simulations. The DMN becomes caught up in visualizing minimovies, which can become quite protracted. Anecdotally, the Hebrew slang for this simulated thinking is loosely translated as "eating movies," and just as with movies, they can be dramatic. As with our preoccupations with thoughts about ourselves and ToM speculations, these scenarios can be wonderfully valuable for preparing for life's challenges, but they can also become overly consuming. Some are remarkably elaborate.

On a trip back from Germany with Nili recently, while we were standing by the carousel waiting for our luggage, being a curious creature, Nili walked right up to the moving belt to watch the luggage spilling onto it. Suddenly, my mind started simulating a scene in which her dress got caught in the belt and she was being dragged by it and how everybody standing around started yelling. I looked around frantically, expecting to find a red emergency button to stop the carousel but could not see one, so I jumped on the moving belt to save her, yanking her dress free. Nili pulled me back to the present by exclaiming that our bags had just appeared. Luckily, my wild scenario didn't happen, but I would have been ready if it had.

Our simulations are certainly not always about catastrophes, though I seem to excel at those. Such dire musings point to why preparing us for what's coming seems to have taken evolutionary precedence over developing a machinery for cherishing the moment. The unfortunate upshot is that by not being in the now more often, we miss so much of what is novel and interesting and could lead to creative ideas and overall enrich our experiences.

Mental Simulations from Associative Elements

The predictions generated by our proactive brains not only are the basis for complicated simulations but lie in the basis of each of our decisions. German philosopher Karl Popper famously said that we let our hypotheses die in our stead. Predictions and simulations (dress rehearsals of the mind), which rely on associations for foundations, help us weigh the possible outcomes of each alternative on a decision "tree" and choose the action that is expected to yield the most desired outcome. Should I stay or should I go now? Choosing a course of action, even just what to have for lunch, involves "running" an internal simulation of the multiple futures that will ensue with each alternative decision: marrying or not (consider Charles Darwin's famous list of the pros and cons of marrying), travel to South America or Southeast Asia, cheesecake or chocolate cake? Each decision is a junction, with at least two options. We run, consciously or not, a quick simulation of the predicted outcomes and the way the alternative experiences will unfold, which we can do because of memory and our past experiences, and we choose the one we want. We can anticipate the response of our spouse if we return home with flowers or alternatively with junk we found on the street and liked; we can foresee the sensation in our mouth, head, and stomach if we choose to eat that chocolate bar; and we can envision the time and money spent compared with the fun that a spontaneous trip would entail. All decisions are basically guided by an expected reward (or punishment) outcome. And we want reward; reward is what steers our actions.

Nadia, our middle ("central") daughter, is a natural-born cognitive neuroscientist, coming up with insights and creative suggestions for experiments for me to try in the lab since she was seven. She came up with a brilliant algorithm for making hard decisions. What she does (and I do, too, now) is to flip a coin between the two options and then observe closely her immediate response to the outcome. Then she chooses between the two based on her reaction to the one that won. It may sound trivial until you try it; I was surprised by how strong a relief or disappointment I could feel when one of the two decisions that seemed comparable just a second ago won. This goes to show that even our best forecast for a certain future is not always valid until the decision actually has to be made, so simulations can get you only so far.

Not all decisions are a result of extended simulations and deliberations. Some decisions are impulsive, spur of the moment, and it is not
clear they go through any simulation before we act on them. Kids are
an excellent example. They do not have enough experience on which
to build simulations yet, nor do they have a developed prefrontal cortex with which to run such simulations. Owing to that underdeveloped
prefrontal cortex, they also lack inhibition and lack understanding of
potential consequences, and they do not engage in predecision deliberations as much. I was taking a dirt-bike path with my son, Naor, one
day, and when we reached a little hill I stopped abruptly to check what
was awaiting on the other side. My son was bummed and in frustration
yelled, "Why, Dad? That's all the fun!" I explained to him that I first
wanted to see that it was safe to jump, to minimize surprises by seeing
what was waiting on the other side of that hill (feel free to think about
it as a metaphorical hill), and to weigh our options in a more informed
manner before we rushed to enjoy the thrill. He thought I was lame, but I
was just using what I have learned in my many more years of experience.

Beyond impulsive decisions, another type of decision that is not preceded by simulations is the more automatic ones. You return from a long
run in the heat, and you know you want something cold to drink right
that moment, and it does not matter if it is water or apple juice. It seems
that there are some obvious needs that do not require a simulation, not
even a decision. It is an automatic response, an association between a
state and an action, which has been thoroughly learned with experience.
It is yet another ingenious aspect of the way our brains work, autom-
atizing whatever has been sufficiently learned so it doesn't need to be
simulated anew each time we encounter it.

But in most decisions, we do use our memory and past experience
to build those predictions and simulations. If you had to imagine the
library in a city you have never visited, or the taste of strawberry jam

mixed for some reason with black pepper, you could have a pretty good idea of what to expect by retrieving and modifying past experiences. We lean on our past to approximate the future. To emphasize this point, try to imagine how life might look after death or how aliens might look. It feels completely fictional, groundless, and fantastic because we do not have real experience on which to base those simulations. At the same time, we have no problem at all imagining a lion with pink tights reading a book in a hammock tied between two palm trees on the moon.

We store our experiences, sometimes earned with blood, sweat, and tears, in memory for the future, but we also store in memory our simulated, imagined experiences as "memory." Simulations are like real experiences, only imagined, and without the bruises of real experience. The powerful characteristic of our brains is that those rich, elaborate, informed simulations can eventually be stored in memory and later be retrieved as a script for our behavior, just as real memory that is based on real experience can. You drive back home in the evening and try to plan your dinner. You retrieve from memory the image of what you had in your fridge when you last saw it in the morning. You think about those ingredients and the recipes of what you know to make, plus the body signals that tell you what you feel like eating. You go over it until you have your entire meal planned. The end result of this simulation, a plan, is then saved in your memory. When you get home, you have a script ready to follow, almost automatically. Scripts can of course be of less boring (but useful) scenarios. You are sitting on a local bus on some exotic road in India. The driver is going fast and to an outsider seems reckless, and the road is curved, so you start thinking about what if the bus rolls over. You think about the possible hit your body will take, what will your head and shoulders hit, and how you could minimize the injury, if it rolled to the left or to the right. You think about the other passengers, how to help them, and how to protect yourself from the loose luggage over your head. Like in many other simulations, this may be far-fetched and the chances of it really happening slim. Nevertheless, if it did happen, you will be the ready passenger.

No matter how many years I have been studying and thinking about this issue, it never ceases to impress me that we can learn from experiences that never happened, learning from our thoughts and imagination.

Simulations can also invoke feelings and emotions associated with the imagined experience, sometimes too reliably. There is an annual scientific meeting I used to attend for many years, taking place in different towns along the gorgeous west coast of the state of Florida. I remember one year, during the flight from Boston to Tampa, I started running in my head what I imagined was going to unfold once I landed, just like every year: pick up my luggage, go to the rental car office, pick up the red convertible Mustang (scientist gone wild . . .), drive a couple of hours, check in at the hotel, unpack, change into running clothes, go run on the beautiful beach for an hour, come back, take a shower, go downstairs to the hotel's nice restaurant, have a delicious meal I know I like with beer, come back to the room, check the scientific program for tomorrow, watch a movie, fall asleep. Sounded like a perfect few hours, only in my mind now after the detailed simulation; it felt like I had already lived it all, and there was no point in actually executing it. So I stayed in bed instead. The realism of simulations could explain why high hopes are so often disappointing: you have already harvested most of the fun during simulation. Low hopes, on the other hand, might leave much to be experienced. What I have learned from Buddhism, however, is that sometimes it is best to have no expectations at all.

Vivid simulations can also serve as a surprising weapon against procrastination and for getting us into action with things we are reluctant to do. Simulations bring events closer to us. I call this process of making things appear more plausible through simulations *mental salivation*. I lie in bed, with zero energy to go out for a run. I then start imagining the upcoming activity in detail: how I put on my running clothes, tie my running shoes, strap my phone to my arm, put the house key in my back pocket, and get out the door; imagining my route and what I know I will be seeing and feeling along the way, and the whole experience suddenly seems more imminent, with no buffers and obstacles between me and actually running. This may be teaching us something important about the link between mental activity and physical action. Indeed, simulating in our mind the process of preparing for an exam improves studying and performance,[3] and mental practice helps novice surgeons to manage stress,[4] to name a few.

A term that used to be highly influential in the study of perception and action, coined by psychologist J. J. Gibson, is *affordance*: to what extent the features of what is in front of you afford a specific action. This principle can guide design for interactions and is applicable not only in the study of perception and action but also in architecture, advertising, product design, and more. And so, simulations that are extra detailed increase the perceived affordance. Running seems much more doable now that I have envisioned the details. Not only do they increase the perceived feasibility of a possibly upcoming event, but simulations also remind us of the feelings and rewards associated with an event, like a postrun high, which add the motivation needed to get up and do it. The design of products, for example, needs to make it easy for a potential customer to see himself using that product, so it should be obvious how the intended action is afforded by the design. In fact, our entire body seems to be working in anticipation. When we are about to bite a piece of lemon or a chocolate bar, our tongue responds with anticipatory salivation, which facilitates the actual experience of taste and subsequently helps chew and swallow.[5] Simulations help us prepare for and embrace upcoming experiences.

Taken together, we understand that memory, in its stored associations, is used as a means for generating predictions; predictions help us proactively prepare and optimize our interaction with the environment, and they are used as the building blocks of mental simulations. But the brain's default network, DMN, and the corresponding wandering mind, does not only concern the future. It is more generally a magnificent apparatus for mental time travel and a platform for diverse thought content.

Mental Time Travel

Palinopsia is a curious neurological disorder where a visual image persists long after the stimulus has vanished. You stare at your dog for a second, move your eyes to the text you were reading, but you still see the dog overlaid on top of the text. This phenomenon can stem from multiple sources, including lesions to the visual cortex, epileptic seizures, and a neuronal overexcitability. It could involve illusions about the environment or internally generated hallucinations, and it could be accompanied by various symptoms, but the result is equally debilitating. Palinopsia it not that common (I was reminded of it recently by my daughter Nadia, who heard a character on the TV show *Teen Wolf* mention it and she got curious), but it does make one appreciate pure perception and the possibly devastating effects of clutter.

Now imagine seeing your world not as two overlaid images like a palinopsia patient, but rather constantly as three unrelated images superimposed on top of each other, like those transparencies on which we used to show slides, or film negatives, of, say, a beach, a conference room, and a close-up face all on top of each other. You want to focus on the face, but those other two images keep distracting you and taking you away from the quality and the details of that face. This is how most of us spend most of our lives, in a complex superposition clutter, yet oblivious. At any given moment, the content of your thought consists of the present (right in front of you), the past (some random reminiscing or a memory that is or is not related in some way to your present), and the future (planning, weighing consequences, or simply worrying), like a Janus face but with three sides. Just think about it, holding in your working memory at the very same time the taste of that chocolate bar in your mouth, the conversation you had with the cashier when you bought it a minute ago, and the workout you will have to do as a result of this chocolate indulgence: pleasure, guilt, images, and words mixed with past, present, and future. How can you be immersed in the present, in life itself, with so much competition and parallel demand on your mental capacities?

The mind's amazing ability for time travel is powerful and can be useful. By being aware of our proclivity to wander in time, and across topics, we should strive to harness it for our best interests. Of course, we need to be able to plan (future) or learn from our mistakes (past), but we do not want it to interfere with our enjoyment of the present. So, mental time travel is both a gift and a curse; it helps us prepare and reminisce, but it also deprives us of the present.

I recently stumbled upon a recording of a big event with a famous, successful, and interesting figure who has been a great promoter of the power of now. He started by saying that he rarely thinks about the past, but I beg to differ. We may not be conscious of our mental time travel, and we may be able to train ourselves to think consciously more about the present, but we cannot even do so much as cross the road without something in our mind referring to past experience and deriving what should be the next step. Nature has decided for us to surf through life by leaning on our accumulated experience. Being always now means not benefiting from your lifetime of experience, as stored in memory and being streamed to you from the top down.

"The price of liberty is eternal vigilance" is a quote I love, often attributed to Thomas Jefferson (1826) as well as to John Philpot Curran (1808). Being exploratory is as close to freedom as I can think, but indeed it entails not only learning and fun adventures but also always being on the lookout and not leaning on memory. Being permanently at this stage of heightened vigilance is both costly and dangerous, so nature's choice for us is well understood. Sure, we can do the metaphorical, or literal, bungee jumping from time to time, but we will not be getting very far if that is our only state.

And about that mental time travel, poet Alberto Caeiro (Fernando Pessoa) has written,

> Live, you say, in the present;
> Live only in the present.
>
> But I don't want the present, I want reality;
> I want things that exist, not time that measures them.
>
> What is the present?
> It's something relative to the past and the future.
> It's a thing that exists in virtue of other things existing.
> I only want reality, things without the present.
>
> I don't want to include time in my scheme.
> I don't want to think about things as present; I want
>   to think of them as things.

In my several Vipassana retreats I have often found myself wondering how these experienced teachers who came from abroad to teach us took care of their traveling arrangements without thinking about the future. Beyond marking your calendar, you need to choose the best itinerary, combine with other plans, think about transportation to and from the airport, what to pack, things you need to finish so that you can afford the time away, and how to be ready for various potential mishaps, such as delays and missed connections, all of which involve memory-based (past) simulations (future). Obviously, we cannot be exclusively in the present at all times, or else the human race would have not made it to the moon or achieved much. Our brain is built for planning and preparing, a proactive brain, so it is both difficult to fight this tendency as well as not always advisable. And even if we could fight planning completely—say, we lived in a cave where all our needs were met by others and we had absolutely nothing to worry about—there would be plenty of planning going on without us being aware. Even just reaching to grasp a glass of water entails executing a "motor plan" that involves optimizing the future upfront. How far, how fast, and with what muscle tension to extend your arm? How much to spread each of your fingers, and how strongly to hold the glass so it neither breaks from the pressure nor drops from your hand? Part of us is always busy with some planning, not all being carried out by the DMN and rather recruiting more dedicated brain areas. The secret is to limit it to certain situations and to certain practicalities. Mindfulness meditation, in that sense, helps minimize the time you spend in the future to what is absolutely necessary and along the way also helps you be mindful (aware) of the planning that is going on in your mind.

Mindwandering, daydreaming, and reverie (in the more psychological therapy context, as used by Thomas Ogden, for example) collectively host multiple types of content. What they all have in common is that these different contents and processes accomplish something useful, and at the same time they all imply you are not on target and not entirely in the present. When you are engaged in a specific and demanding task, such as working on a crossword, driving a sports car, or making love, your mind is busy with the activity at hand, for each of which the brain has dedicated areas, networks, and patterns of neuronal activity. During those times, the default network will be less filled with mindwandering content. That said, most everyday tasks are easy enough for us that they leave some mental resources unused, and this reserve is used for wandering, thought unrelated to what you are doing right now.

Taken together, the occupation of the brain's default network with mindwandering on its various flavors is not binary, but rather a spectrum from high to low, and the possibilities along this spectrum include the following: you are engaged in a most consuming task, and thus there are no resources left to indulge in any mindwandering at all, even for necessary background planning; you are engaged in a medium-demand task that leaves resources for some mindwandering, default action; you are busy with nothing at all, like in the shower or a traffic jam, so all or at least most of your default network is busy with task-independent spontaneous mindwandering thoughts; or the all too frequent alternative where you are supposed to be busy with a task, such as listening or watching, but instead your mind has drifted. When you daydream in class, it means even the one task you have, listening, has been hijacked by your brain's desire to mentally travel. Comedian Steven Wright once quipped, "I was trying to daydream, but my mind kept wandering." The joke was funny because we all know that during daydreaming, our thoughts wander all over the place. Task or not, our mind is racing. If not aiming toward achieving a specified goal, your mind will be daydreaming, fantasizing, ruminating, or obsessing, reminiscing on something from the past, or worrying about something in the future. One thing is for certain, our mind is never idle.

CHAPTER SEVEN

THE LOSS OF NOVELTY

Human beings are born with an attraction to the new. It seems that advertisers have known this all along. Researchers who study child development have found that even babies show a clear preference for looking at an object that is new to them over one they have seen before. This early preference for novelty is so strong and reliable that we use it as a way to study recognition in preverbal babies. For example, if we've shown a baby a tomato and then show her a tomato again along with a cucumber, she will look at the cucumber, and this tells us that she recognized the tomato as familiar. Her brain orients her to the novelty. This explains why infants could spend such a long time checking out a paper clip.

The New Serves the Future

Why would we be so attracted to novelty? The answer has to do with the real role of memory in our being. We want to be able to predict what is next, to be optimally prepared for the future, and to generate those predictions we lean on memory, approximating the future from our past experience. That which is new is that which we have not anticipated, so we inspect it and plug our discovery into our memory database to ready ourselves for however we may encounter it again in the future. Being attracted to novelty and swallowing in everything new allows us to expand the set of situations for which we can prepare. This is why attraction to novelty, regardless of whether we like it, which we often do not, is so ingrained in us. Better preparation means better chances of surviving and succeeding.

How do we draw on our past experience for predictions in everyday life? According to our *proactive brain* framework, when we are in a certain situation, we immediately strive to find an analogy to similar situations from the past.[1] I remember showing my parents Boston or San Francisco streets for their first time, how it struck me that my father kept comparing places to others he had seen elsewhere in the past. Or how we compare a person we meet for the first time to someone we already know. A new actor enters the scene, and immediately your brain works to find someone that this person reminds you of. The brilliant vision scientist David Marr said that the purpose of our visual system is to understand what is where.[2] Right then, walking on new streets with my parents, it dawned on me that the first question the brain asks with everything it encounters is actually not "What is this?" but rather "What is this *like*?" By making a quick analogy, connecting the input with existing memory, we gain access to an ocean of knowledge and associations that have been accumulated through experience. You see a new type of chair, and even though you have never seen this one before you still recognize it as a chair because it shares a sufficient number of features (legs, support, and so forth) with the category of chairs that you already know. Once this connection has been made, you know its function, its approximate weight, and even its approximate price, and all that without having seen this specific item before in your life. Our ability to interpret and to predict our environment depends on our past. This is a pretty powerful capability of our mind, which tends to be underappreciated because we do it so often and so seamlessly during our day, looking at something we have never seen before yet immediately knowing so much about it.

It makes sense that evolution selected for our attraction to the novel, because things we aren't familiar with and haven't anticipated might pose a threat to us. In fact, our minds by default interpret the new as dangerous. One Boston winter afternoon, I was sitting in the backyard when suddenly I sensed in my right hip what felt like a pointed and deep stab from a knife or a mean needle. Horror engulfed me at that part of a second that it took me to examine the area and see a drop of water. A freezing-cold drop from a melting icicle above me found its way between my sweater and my jeans. This is how dramatic interpretation without a prior expectation could be. The vast majority of our sensations, moment by moment, day by day, are expected to some extent. It's hard to believe, and it makes it sound like we have predictable and boring lives, but this is the omnipresent power of using our experience to anticipate perceptions, responses, or the end of a movie.

But this little icicle anecdote also demonstrates our inability to just feel, to sense without attaching a meaning. I sensed the sensation, and my brain was racing for an explanation. Why it chose such a dramatic cause for the sensation is another matter, but it did. If we were able to just sense, like mindfulness and other meditation practices encourage us to do, I might have just observed that sensation without panicking. But this is not us. I did not predict this perception, and I could not merely sense without interpretation, so my brain attached to it a meaning.

Recall the Haro figures from the previous chapter. Ambiguous items remain ambiguous until contextual information disambiguates their identity and meaning. An ambiguous hairdryer looks like a drill in the context of a workshop and like a hairdryer in the context of a bathroom or hair salon.[3] Similarly, the word "bank" is interpreted as a riverbank when appearing after a word related to the context of a river, like "water," and interpreted as a money bank if preceded by a word such as "save."[4] But until contextual information becomes available for disambiguation, we gravitate toward negative interpretations, just like in my icicle drama.[5]

Fitting new input into old templates is an ingenious mechanism for maximizing meaning and certainty in our lives. However, there is a serious flip side to this ingenuity. The trade-off is clear: we either strive to protect ourselves by attaching meaning to our sensations and responding according to that understanding as soon as possible, or suspend interpretation and just feel, but then expose ourselves to potential threats. When to do what is a matter of awareness and of practice.

Perceiving Memory

As we grow, since early childhood, we accumulate experience and knowledge with exposure to the physical world around us. We gradually develop a library in memory of how the world, things, and people behave; how best to respond; what we like; what we want; what we fear; and so on. We constantly strive to enrich this library, as reflected by what attracts our attention and what from each experience remains in our memory after the experience has passed. When we encounter a new experience—a situation, a stimulus, an image, a text, a conversation, a person, a movie, a restaurant—we deploy this library to help us interpret and respond to that experience in a way that seems optimal. This influence of our existing templates on new experience is exerted "top-down." Experience-based expectations are a powerful way for us to understand our world quickly and efficiently, but they are not the only ingredient in the mix. Preconceptions, desires, and biases are also streaming down from high-level cortical regions and dominate what otherwise could have been a veridical, accurate comprehension of life around us.

In the philosophy of Immanuel Kant, there is a distinction between how we perceive things in the world and what he called "the thing-in-itself." There is the physical truth about the features of the object of our attention, the thing itself, and there is the way it appears to us. The thing-in-itself pertains to the actual properties of the observed object or phenomena—Is it red? Is it curved? Is it big? Is it far?—regardless of who observes it or whether it is being observed at all. As Kant puts it, "And we indeed, rightly considering objects of sense as mere appearances, confess thereby that they are based upon a thing in itself, though we know not this thing as it is in itself but only know its appearances, viz., the way in which our senses are affected by this unknown something."[6]

The thing-in-itself is the truth, while perception is our individual-ized truth. This is how we live and how we have been living all along. Kant's views were supported and extended in intriguing ways by German philosopher and fascinating pessimist Arthur Schopenhauer in his four volumes of *The World as Will and Representation*, where representation is the appearance and the will stands for the thing-in-itself. Our mind, yet again, makes us really confident with our subjective perceptions. In many airplanes, critical parameters such as the gas level or the altitude of the airplane have two independent indicators for each. After a few rolls and some confusion of what is up and what is down, the pilot might be so convinced that her perception of the airplane's orientation is more accurate than that of the indicator that they installed a second one to make it clear to the pilot that the thing-in-itself is the indicator, not the subjective and volatile perception.

We rely more and more on what we already know and less and less on what there is to perceive anew. The more experiences we have, the more we begin to interpret our moment-to-moment living through the lens of our memory. Somewhat sadly, beyond a certain age, novelty is rare, and most everyday situations have been experienced in one way or another already in our past. We become less and less exploratory of our surroundings and progressively find them more familiar, so not in need of close observation. Been there, done that. Our beautiful tendency to pay close attention to everything around us, to be open and absorbed by what we are seeing, hearing, and feeling, inexorably dissipates.

We look for the expected so much that we see it even when it's not there. This has been strikingly demonstrated by numerous studies with what is known as the Kanizsa triangle. People shown this figure see a white triangle in the middle, but that's an optical illusion. The three Pac-Man creatures give the impression of three angles aligned with each other, so our brain completes the rest. We see a triangle where we expect a triangle. So much so that even neurons at the earliest regions of the visual cortex show response to the imaginary lines as if they were real.[7] Gradually, perception becomes more a process of reassuring expectations from memory than a veridical response to the features that are out there.

Neuroscience has worked out that what's happening here is that the prefrontal cortex is feeding top-down information about what the object is expected to be that tells the neurons in the earlier stages of visual cortex how to anticipate it, rather than those neurons being allowed to send exclusively unfiltered observatory information to the temporal cortex, where identities are eventually determined for us. Otherwise, if it were only bottom-up information that drives our perception, we would have seen three Pac-Mans, without that illusory white triangle, as it is. But our perceptions are a mixture of top-down information from within and bottom-up information from the senses. Ideally, the bottom-up information provides the physical properties of our surroundings, and the top-down processes would attach meaning to these perceptions. But as we have seen, we sometimes take our prior knowledge and our generalizations too far.

A Flexible Mind Can Harden Your Heart

On my morning jog not long ago, I ran into Quentin Tarantino: Quentin Tarantino, in Tel Aviv, walking in the park, on a path surrounded by oblivious young mothers and young babies, litter, crows, and an environment that in all respects is very remote from Hollywood Hills. In our ever more surreal world, it seems we can accept just about anything. Tarantino is one of my favorite directors of all time. Yet I was not that ecstatic about this encounter, though of course excited, just because I had already run into him in our neighborhood café a couple of weeks earlier and imposed on him my childish-fan introduction. Having seen him just once before was already enough to markedly temper my reaction to the greatness of my privilege: our adaptive mind.

Is adaptability a desirable trait? Sure, in the recent pandemic it has helped us all quickly adjust to a new routine that involves masks, social distancing, and heightened hygiene, but not all changes in circumstances justify getting used to. We do not want to adapt to the presence of lions or snakes when hiking in the jungle, but rather to remain alert and on the lookout for suspicious signs. Similarly, I do not want to get used to the fact that the beautiful Mediterranean beach is a ten-minute walk from my apartment; I prefer to be excited about this proximity to paradise every day.

As we have already seen, our brain is wired for novelty; it is tuned to what is unfamiliar and unexpected, so that we can survive, learn, and flourish. This is why our brains are less and less excited with increased familiarity. A new stimulus, be it the first mango you taste, the first drop of blood you see, or your first roller-coaster ride, elicits maximal response from your neurons. More neurons will respond, and stronger, to a novel event than when the novelty wears off. With less neuronal activation comes a reduced release of neurotransmitters such as dopamine, which is the chemical that helps us experience the rush both from pleasure and from the novel. Familiarity, in most circumstances, is less rewarding.

The same mechanism that helps us acclimate to the possibility of earthquakes or seasonal hurricanes, once we have experienced a couple, is the mechanism that makes us enjoy *Pulp Fiction* a little less the second time, and it is the reason we are unfortunately able to eat our favorite ice cream mindlessly. Getting used to the good is not simply restricted to ice cream, however. Relationships are jaded and careers end because of our weariness of the familiar. It becomes clear that our ability to tolerate the bad stuff in our life is due to our quick adaptation, but also that this powerful gift to acclimate comes at the price of enjoying the good stuff much less when it becomes familiar: a painful trade-off.

Not only that: even for negative circumstances, it is not clear that adapting is always in our best interest. Do we really want to get used to all kinds of bad? An abusive spouse, motor vehicle fatalities, oppressing other people, and other injustices are just a few examples of situations where people adapt to tolerate when they should not. Hearing about a prime minister who incites racism and divides his nation with his comments, a president who cheats and lies, or a tech giant that is selling our personal information was shocking when the first news stories came about, but not anymore. It seems that with familiarity through repetition, we have gotten used to views and actions that would have shocked our parents. But we simply sigh and flip the page.

Can we trick this evolutionary trade-off? Can we exert voluntary control such that we could, by choice, enjoy the familiar every time as if it were fresh (can you imagine how life would be if every kiss felt like your first kiss?) and resist adaptation when it should be avoided? Just like we do not get near food that previously caused us food poisoning, we should remain as averse to corrupt leaders, abusive relations, and chronically delayed technicians as we were the first time.

Like in many challenges of the mind, mere awareness is already a good part of the solution. In extreme cases, a force outside our own mind needs to remind us when we have gotten used to the wrong norms; the #MeToo movement being a good recent example. But in most other cases, think of that kid who asks a question that makes you embarrassed that you have never wondered about it yourself, like why the lake is blue one day and green the next day, or where the phrase "rule of thumb" came from (look it up—another instance of standards that shouldn't have been). You can be that kid by occasionally revisiting the things to which you have become numb.

Beyond those cases where we want to remain honest with ourselves by not getting used to information that does not fit our authentic values, we need to adopt a strategy of selective attention or selective adaptation. To some it comes naturally. My late grandfather was famous for stopping an extended family dinner only to make us all contemplate for a long minute something like the fork. What a great invention, and how could we ever eat without it? Not to mention the gusto with which he cherished his after-nap coffee every day, for decades. Not everybody is so lucky to have a genuine and lasting appreciation of the mundane and the familiar, though my students, who find it amusing that I can burst into their office with astonishment that I sent an email to a friend in Australia and got a response within a couple of minutes, are convinced that this appreciative trait is genetic.

Beyond frequent awareness to our adaptations, there are other ways one can nourish the ability to continue to see familiar environments in new, fresh light. Meditation is one example, but the basic principle is not tied to a specific practice. Our mind constantly refers back to memory so that past experiences can guide our future actions in an informed manner. As we saw, this is hugely helpful, but it becomes an obstacle when trying to enjoy our present experience. Evolution, understandably, has prioritized our survival over our ability to appreciate the present. So, to reclaim what's ours, we need to put in a little fight. Shutting off our constant reference to memory and past experience so that we can enjoy that flower in front of us each time like it is a novelty does not come naturally, but it is possible. Disconnect from your memory whenever you can observe yourself falling into old templates, if only to revaluate the things you have mindlessly adapted to along the way.

CHAPTER EIGHT

TEMPLATES OF MIND AND THE LIMITS OF BOUNDARIES

W E LOOK FOR THE FAMILIAR SO THAT WE CAN IGNORE IT IN OUR QUEST for the new. To do that, we give a meaningful label to the things we already know when we encounter them: a flower, a car, food. But our need for meaning goes beyond labeling the familiar.

Our Desperate Need for Meaning

Sensory deprivation tanks, or isolation tanks, are dark, completely silent tanks filled with saltwater at skin temperature, where one floats without hearing, without seeing, and without feeling much. This may sound relaxing, but generally the experience of being disconnected from the external physical world is so unnatural to us that sensory deprivation tanks were used in the past as a form of torture. Mindwandering, with all the benefits that it confers, is not enough for us; we need an external world, and we need it to be meaningful.

Our need for the external world is perhaps most oddly demonstrated by a phenomenon called *the prisoner's cinema*, which pertains to reports by prisoners who have been confined to darkness, as well as reports by truck drivers, pilots, and those who practice intense forms of meditation (there is something unnerving about the same reports coming from truck drivers and intense meditators . . .), of seeing imagined lights and colors that sometimes have abstract form but sometimes are more concrete. Some have even found similarities between these reports and the Neolithic cave paintings.[1] One prevalent explanation has to do with *phosphenes* (loosely translated as "light-show" from the Greek), the phenomenon of seeing light without external simulation, which could occur by mechanical pressure to the eye (like when rubbing your eyes and seeing lights) or by spontaneous activity in the visual cortex. There are several other demonstrations in this family, like the *Charles Bonnet syndrome*, where blind people experience complex visual hallucinations, or the *musical ear syndrome*, where individuals with hearing loss experience auditory musical hallucinations. Many of these phenomena and explanations are based on personal reports, and as such are not always scientifically characterized, but they do attest to the system's need for an external world, even if it has to be imagined.

Our mental life, personal as it might feel, is shaped by the world around us. It is also the other way around: our inner world affects the way we interpret the world outside. We translate the world from reality to our own "reality." Almost as a necessity, we interpret and dress incoming information with familiar meaning to think we understand it or just to feel better able to handle our life by putting things into existing "boxes," templates, in our memory. Familiar makes us comfortable.

Just like we cannot not name a sound or label an odor or categorize a taste we are sensing, it is impossible for us to not interpret a situation in terms that are familiar to us. This is why many feel aversion to abstract art and other formations that resist interpretation; we need to be able to put names and labels on what we encounter. When my middle daughter, Nadia, was a toddler, in my arms, looking at a Pollock piece in a museum, her reaction was "He needs to clean after himself"; she found a label quickly. A decade later, she asked to be tested for attention deficit hyperactivity disorder (all our three kids inherited that gift from me). I initially said there was no need because I would not let her take medications, so she would have to manage just like I have. Her response was that she did not want medications, just a diagnosis label so that she knows what she has, can put it in a box, and live with more certainty onward. Look at the clouds, and see if you can avoid giving names to the shapes you see in them, what they look like. Even though your brain knows these are clouds of dry air and water and ice particles, it nevertheless cannot calm down before it says to itself that this blob looks like an elephant standing on a basketball. As Hannah Arendt nicely put it: "The need of reason is not inspired by the quest for truth but by the quest for meaning." We want meaning more than we want truth.

Putting Things in Boxes

Individuals can be born with cataracts so bad that they are basically congenitally blind. After the procedure to remove such cataracts was developed, the life of many improved dramatically. See the humanitarian and scientific work of Pawan Sinha, of the Massachusetts Institute of Technology, in India for some inspiration. Beyond the medical and well-being aspects involved, this procedure, which turns a blind person into a sighted person, has provided a unique platform for testing some long-standing philosophical questions. One is the *Molyneux's problem* of whether a blind person who used to sense her world through hearing and touching will be able, if she suddenly gains sight, to distinguish between shapes such as a sphere and a cube only by looking. The answer curiously seems to be no. What is more interesting and relevant here, however, is the personal reports of the newly sighted, and of those observing them, about how their visual perception of the world unfolds over time after the procedure. There are both deep frustration and extreme awe (depending on cases and on personal dispositions), but there are also fascinating descriptions of how the world looks for someone with no previous experience with vision. They initially, for the first few days typically, do not see objects; they see color patches instead. A strawberry is just a red pattern touching a smaller green pattern: no name, no associations, no memories. Even shadows are just darker patches to them, instead of providing depth and illumination information that the rest of us typically extract from a shadow. They see the world like infants, before they are taught to attach names to those patches. They see the world from the bottom up, from edges, textures, colors, and motion upward. They do not project from the top down meanings, associations, and expectations like we do. They see it as it is.

This may sound like a curse, but in fact it may be achieving one tall order of Buddhism practice, one that even experienced meditators have a hard time achieving on a regular basis, the one where you are challenged to try to listen to sounds like an approaching train or the meow of a cat and not give them a name or a category. In my laboratory, where we often study questions related to human vision, we wanted at some point to create visual stimuli that do not look like any object, meaningless objects. It turned out to be impossible. We can't stop our mind from giving objects their names. And when they are not actual objects, we give them the name of the object closest to them in our imagination (the ever-intriguing phenomenon of *pareidolia*). We cannot perceive physical stimulations as just such. We cannot unmango a mango. Yet this is the ultimate goal (or at least one of them) in meditation training. Alan Watts, in his brilliant fifteen-minute guided meditation "Awakening the Mind" encourages his listeners to do that. He even goes further to ask that we treat not only outside sounds as nameless noise but also our inner thoughts as noise, until the inner world and the outer world become one. This is according to Watts, and I cannot say I have ever gotten close to this myself in my minimal practice so far. Nevertheless, we can see how this also connects to the discussion about the self and how meditation pushes us to eliminate the separation we have between our self and our external world. When talking about the self in Chapter 4, eliminating the self sounded theoretical and perhaps impossible to accomplish. Resisting labeling, unnatural as it may sound, already offers a practical application toward the worthy goal of dissolving artificial borders separating us from our world. Watts has put it nicely: "We suffer from the delusion that the entire Universe is held in order by the categories of human thought, fearing that if we do not hold onto them with the utmost tenacity, everything will vanish into chaos."[2]

Ofer Lellouche is a luminary Israeli French sculptor and a friend. He told me once how he noticed that in his drawing classes, people have a hard time drawing a collection of leaves and stems in his studio as he asks them to do. There is a big pot, with multiple plants in it. What he asks them to do is not to draw the entire thing but just a specific imaginary square at the middle of this array. It consists of a random mess of stems and leaves going in different directions, obscuring parts of each other, eventually connecting to different plants. His students, like the rest of us would, have difficulty disconnecting their drawing from their prior knowledge about the origin, destination, and affiliation of every line within that square, such that they draw plants in complete parts that connect to each other, disregarding parts of other plants that might be occluding, as well as continue beyond the designated frame. Their drawing corresponds more to a schema they have in mind than to the actual information in that square. This is related to but not fully explained by a phenomenon we call in psychology *boundary extension*, first characterized and termed by Helene Intraub and colleagues. In boundary extension, people are asked to remember a picture they are shown, such as a bunch of trash cans leaning against a picket fence, with the lids and the top of the fence trimmed, not shown in the picture. When asked to redraw from memory, people tend to complete the drawing (of the cans and fence in this example) so that it includes completed objects. It is hard for us to remember partial objects. This is reminiscent of what bothers some in French cinema, where often we see a period in someone's life, with no clear beginning or ending, and nothing major happening in between, just life.

Interestingly, we do this not only with individual identities but also with relations between items. When we show participants in our experiments pictures of two objects simultaneously, as I did with Yael Afiki in my lab, they cannot help but try to connect them somehow. When you see objects that are obviously related to each other, like a chair and a table, a dog and a bone, or a doctor and a nurse, you see the connection and you move on. But if you see things that have no direct link, like a pear and a saxophone, a tank and a dreidel, or a stapler and a pine tree, your mind nevertheless works feverishly on finding a satisfying association between them. And if you do try to move on, you find out, or not (it is not always conscious), that a part of your mind is still digging, obsessing, and ruminating. You may notice that you do not have all your mental capacities available for what is next, because some of it is still consumed by that background effort to find an associative connection.[3] We seek coherence, and meaning, by connecting to what is known and thereby feel more certain about our model of the world and our confidence in our understanding of our environment.

In my friend Sasha's apartment in Jaffa, the projector and the stereo are always on. He plays progressive music that is always new and in parallel streams random YouTube videos on the big wall. At first I thought he was genius in his ability to match them so that they go so well together; how does he do it so fast? But then I realized the magic is happening inside my head and the heads of others in the room. Unbeknownst to us, we work to find connections until things seem to be related and we can settle. And once we do, we marvel ("How is it possible that this Russian rap song is such a perfect soundtrack for that old Japanese animation?"), not realizing that it was not Sasha (who is a brilliant and immensely successful photographer) but our brain. We do the same in higher-level phenomena in our lives: unsolved businesses, "issues," traumas, puzzling human interactions, unmet desires, and so on. We need to settle them with connections to memory and meaning, or else they tax our mental resources by repeatedly coming back.

Buddhist practitioners strive to be able to look at a flower and not call it a flower, not put it in a drawer just yet, as philosophers do with their tendency for what seems like everlasting examination. How I wish I could suspend my craving for reaching a bottom line, a name, or a conclusion, whatever it might be. I remember diving in Sorrento last summer with my son, Naor. We took a course with a great local Italian guide. At some point she grabbed my leg from behind, calling for my attention, only to tell me to slow down. I then realized my son was exploring the reef patiently (apparently, his ADHD is better curbed than mine), whereas I took it as if it were an underwater swimming competition. Moving forward constantly, like I wanted to get somewhere. But there was no destination; diving was right here in front of me. Where was I trying to go? Another lesson. A bottom line, as in naming a sound or searching for a definite answer, is akin to chasing a finish line, some elusive goal that "must" be met before we feel we can move on to the next. Life as connecting one goal achieved with the next, and the next, and so on, piling up achievements. It is like at the carnival, where you collect as many tickets as possible for all the successes you have had at the various games, to only redeem them for a big prize at the end. Is there really a big prize at the end?

Fenced Categories

We think in categories, and we have to place everything we encounter in a familiar box. What is "ordinary" is determined by what we already know and demarcated. Reality has to fit into preexisting templates in our brain, or we see it as strange, weird, abnormal. (Indeed, kids seem to call everything that is new to them "weird.") The moment we open a little, let ourselves deviate from arbitrary borders, these templates become flexible, and an opportunity to learn and grow ensues. But that opening part is not easy.

It is a common and beautiful tradition in Israel to buy flowers for the Shabbat (Saturday). My friend Yair (or was it my dear Oren?) once told me how one Friday he asked the florist to wrap together two types of flowers that he liked. When the lady told him that these flowers do not go together, he said, "Tie them together and they will." For long months afterward, I kept wondering why that simple exchange had captivated me so much. Now I know that my fascination developed because this little story reflects mental flexibility that only a few of us are lucky to possess, and that it is a clear manifestation of our deep need for clarity, borders, and rules. Since then, I play with borders in my life, weighing the pros and cons of strict versus flexible categorical fences at different intersections where I need to choose between what I want and what is expected.

For the past year I have been living in a round house, an igloo in the middle of the Middle East. This is related to another line of research in my lab, showing that people prefer curved contours[4] and round spaces.[5] I love seeing the reactions of friends and family visiting for the first time. "OMG, this is really round!" laughing awkwardly with clear confusion and puzzlement on their faces for an extended duration until they get used to the novelty. Working against the hardwired templates of experience and conventions in our brain is not easy: what is good and what is bad, what is right and what is wrong, what is pretty and what is not, what is cool and what is hot. We are accustomed to templates in memory. It is easier for us to accept what is predictable. Deviations take us out of balance. But every new scenario, new attempt, new exposure makes something new possible. Keeping our mind open means keeping the borders between templates and categories more permeable than they usually are. The word "queer" literally means questionable and suspicious. It is hard to believe that this is what society used to call gay people. But what is widely perceived as strange changes into normal over time and exposure. The first time we hear that a big country just elected a thirtysomething person as its prime minister or president, we find it impossible to believe. How could a thirtysomething run a country? But as time passes, the initial shock turns into curiosity, and next we get used to the idea. The second time a country elects a thirtysomething, it seems completely normal. We have updated our templates and can contain what previously seemed crazy and not within the realm of things we would predict as now completely reasonable. "Weird" becomes "normal" once it is familiar.

We categorize to have meaning and thus feel some subjective certainty that we know what is going on and that we are in control. Not feeling pressure to fit new things into old templates requires being able to tolerate uncertainty. Tolerance for uncertainty comes in an exploratory state of mind, where one is open, curious, broad, creative, and in a good mood, just like kids, who, luckily for them, indeed do not care much about borders. Borders, rules, and categories come from the prefrontal cortex, and theirs is far from having matured yet. For us to emulate this state, we need to find a way to shut off our prefrontal cortex on demand.

Trade-Offs in Brain and Behavior

Rules and templates are important in many respects of human behavior, but not in all. We need to be reminded of when they are good and when adhering to them is less desirable, and aware of the fact that at least to some extent, the choice is in our hands. Then we can apply the best strategy for each situation.

Such trade-offs, like when we should and when we should not follow rules and fit the world into templates, are common in the brain, and they are a manifestation of adaptability, versatility, and power. A related example is the trade-off between exploratory behavior, where we are open to novelty and to uncertainty to satisfy our urge to learn and grow, versus exploitatory behavior, where we prefer the familiar and thinking and behaving based on existing "scripts" of what we already know and expect. The exploration-versus-exploitation trade-off is a recurring theme and an ongoing battle for most of us. Do we let the sensory input guide our experience, or will we be lured to the ease of using memory of previous tried experiences? While where we are on the exploratory-exploitatory continuum is usually determined by our state of mind; it is not out of our volition.

Finally, there is also the trade-off mentioned throughout: the brain tool for survival that is at the same time an obstacle for experiencing life. The advantage of top-down streams of previous experience turns into an awful curse. How can we ever enjoy the present if we are built to constantly connect to the past and prepare for the future? But our brains have not evolved for mindfulness. Fun is possible only for those who survive.

Of course, if you are in the jungle, you would trade the ability to enjoy the infinite beauty of a flower for the ability to generate predictions and use your existing knowledge to stay safe. But, on the other hand, when you are in a safe environment, you would rather silence your top-down machinery and just let things come to you as they are. Alas, you cannot. You are programmed to survive, and reprogramming exploitatory behavior to exploratory behavior when survival is not at stake would not happen easily.

Our Tiny Window of Flexibility

You and that new guy are going to a restaurant for your first date ever. Just before they bring the check, he goes to the restroom and you are left to pay. That moment your brain marked him as "cheap," and he is going to have to work really hard for you to change your mind (assuming you stay together). Even if he insists on paying for all your next restaurant meals together, you will not change your mind so easily. One would think our brains average evaluations across similar incidents, so this guy stops being seen as cheap already on your second date. And you would think that learning is a gradual process, where memory keeps being updated linearly and every new piece of information is assigned an equal weight and helps you make your inner representations of the world balanced. But this is far from being the case. The first encounter matters much more than all the others.

This represents an intriguing paradox. On the one hand, we create new templates, or views, blazingly fast. One incident, one brief presentation, and we have a new template in mind. But, on the other hand, although these new templates are formed instantaneously, it is enough for them to be awfully rigid. We hang on to our just-recently formed templates and are reluctant to update them, expand them, or keep their boundaries flexible and dynamic. It seems that it would have been better to think carefully and await further observations before we are to form a view and a template that is going to remain rigid with us for the long term. But we don't.

Why can't we remain open? What's the downside of simply updating our representations constantly? One downside is that we need to have stable representations, thus fixed and less malleable. But these representations also need to be refined with new information. It is just like when a child sees the first car in her life, she thinks to herself a car has four wheels and windows and it is blue. But the next car is red, and the child realizes cars have windows and four wheels but they can come in different colors. Representation updated. Less top-down dictations from the prefrontal cortex, more flexible learning. These conflicting needs are called *pattern separation* and *pattern completion* in our less intuitive jargon.

The paradox of initial flexibility followed by rigidity is parallel to the trade-off between exploration and exploitation mentioned above. To be in exploration mode means all your antennae are in receiving mode, while anxiety and nervousness of the new and the uncertain take a backseat. Exploitation mode, however, means you choose your actions so as to keep surprises to a minimum. Naturally, not much learning occurs in exploitation of the familiar, but it is more beneficial for survival. Most of us do not have to worry about surviving predators and other life-threatening sources too often, but our brains still choose exploitation mode much more often than they do exploration. And to connect back to our dating couple in the restaurant, our first interaction is done under exploration mode, when we are open to being impressed, one way or another. But that window of opportunity to influence is stunningly brief. Very quickly, we turn back to our default state of exploitation, leaning on what that swift window of exploration has imprinted on us. First we open the window briefly so that we can create a new template, and then it is both stable and rigid.

Not being able to leave the channels of exploration and impression open for long is related to our difficulty to avoid attaching a name to a sound or to a random blob. First impression is the window of how long we can tolerate living without a meaningful label, in uncertainty. Being in an exploitatory mode serves our need for certainty, as well as our desperate desire for meaning. And this is not a coincidence: we need meaning chiefly because of our need for certainty. It may seem that the search for meaning stems from curiosity that we want to satisfy, but curiosity is just the drive for getting at the meaning, and meaning is the information required for getting at certainty.

Curiosity ➤ Meaning ➤ Certainty.

CHAPTER NINE

BREADTH OF THOUGHT, CREATIVITY, AND MOOD

BEING CREATIVE COMES WITH BEING CURIOUS, AND BOTH ARE TIGHTLY linked with how our minds wander. What may be less intuitive is that how creative we are affects our mood and vice versa. It was as I was learning about the link between associative mindwandering and creativity that I stumbled upon a finding in an area of research remote to mine that led to my connection of the breadth of our thinking with elevating our mood.

One day I was catching up on a general psychology journal I sometimes peruse and happened on an article in which the authors mentioned in passing that people who suffer from depression have a hard time taking context into account. Because I had done so much work on how context is represented, activated, and utilized by our minds, I was intrigued. What would our ability to see what's around us have to do with our mood? I decided to delve into how our brain functioning might explain the link, beginning with researching the causes of depression.

As a newcomer to the field, I was struck by the strong connection between *rumination*—that persistent cyclical thinking pattern that keeps surrounding the same topic—and depression, which had long been established but was fresh to me. What particularly caught my attention is that rumination is so narrowly focused. It is a highly constricted form of mindwandering, heavily dominated by a focus on negative events of the past and on the self. A bout of rumination might begin by your mind wandering to an unpleasant remark you made to a friend at dinner the night before and how you regret it. You become intensely focused on how you've hurt her feelings and how she must be upset with you and how others at the table probably think you were a jerk, and you begin cycling through these thoughts over and over again. They lead back to the same place, as though your mind has been put in a cage. In fact, rumination is such a vicious circle that ruminating about an event that wasn't initially particularly negative eventually makes us feel negatively about it. Another way rumination can depress our mood is by fixating on some possible scary future happening, in which case it leads to anxiety rather than depression. Just like trying to not think of white bears makes us think about them even more, trying to get rid of ruminations and intruding thoughts only exacerbates their presence.

The narrow scope of ruminative mindwandering gave me an idea. What if broadly associative mindwandering has the opposite effect on mood, making us feel happier?

Mood for Thought

Feeling really great does not happen often enough. But wanting to feel better is not an indulgence. Mood influences every aspect of our well-being, every thought and every action. Indeed, mood's reach goes far beyond our ups and downs; its influence ranges from depression and anxiety to cardiovascular disease, psychological resilience, cognitive performance, aging, and longevity. Nevertheless, our knowledge of the mechanisms underlying mood has been limited. This lack of understanding, coupled with the cardinal role of mood in our lives, explains why so many resort to unwanted habits such as drugs and alcohol to regulate mood.

In clinical cases, such as major depression, mood is treated with chemicals, psychotherapy, or even, in the most extreme cases, electrical stimulation to the brain. Most of us, however, are okay; we have accepted the mood roller coaster as it is. We go about our lives believing, even if not consciously, that mood is something that is inflicted on us. But is our mood really out of our control? This false belief stems from the fact that mood typically cannot be traced back to a specific event. Unlike emotions, the source of a certain mood cannot always be pinpointed and thus has somewhat of a mysterious feel to it. But our new knowledge now affords a more realistic perception of mood, along with potential ways to optimize it.

A breakthrough idea of mood research is the realization that how we think can affect how we feel. The pattern of thinking, independent of its content—positive, neutral, or negative—can directly influence our mood. It has been known for a while that the other direction of influence exists: how we feel affects how we think. People in a good mood tend to be more creative and better at solving problems that require insight and "aha!" solutions and have access to more unusual information in memory than people in a negative mood. For example, if people are asked to name a means of transportation, the typical response will be "car." A person in a positive mood, however, is more likely to respond more originally with "elevator" or "camel" to the same question. Indeed, it is hard to imagine a creative advertising brainstorming session with depressed copywriters. More important to our well-being, however, is the opposite direction, the potential to improve mood by changing thinking style.

It is easily recognized that our mind is associative. One thing leads to another, usually in a coherent and rapid manner. Strawberries might lead you to think about the Beatles, which lead you to John Lennon, assassination, JFK, president, election, and so on. The hypothesis my lab has put forth is that mood is directly influenced by how broadly associative our thinking pattern is. I will get into some of the many ways we have tested and supported this hypothesis, showing that broad and uninhibited thinking improves mood, whereas a narrow thinking pattern degrades mood. Indeed, rumination is the hallmark not only of clinical depression but also of other psychiatric disorders that involve mood, such as anxiety, addiction, post-traumatic stress disorder, and more.

In a paper titled "The Units of Thought," we showed that, as philosophers and others have argued for many years, the brain is an association machine and, we maintain, a predictive organ.[1] The brain proactively and constantly generates predictions to anticipate what is next. The foundation of those predictions is associations. You see a beach chair, and your mind immediately anticipates also a beach umbrella with high probability because they are associated with each other and thus activated in our brain simultaneously. These predictions are not always that specific; you see a terrified face on someone, and you immediately become alarmed because this makes you anticipate a source of threat in the area—not specific, but a threat nevertheless.

What happens to a mind that is not as actively and broadly associative? Such a mind does not generate predictions and thus cannot anticipate future outcomes, optimal plans, and the intentions of others. Living in a constant state of such uncertainty breeds anxiety and over time often results in depression. Even without worries about the past or the future, not being broadly associative means being "stuck" in thoughts, ruminating. Indeed, the structure, function, and communication pattern within the cortical network mediating associative activation, which means also in the DMN, are seriously compromised in mood disorders.

We addressed, with Eiran Harel, Robert Tennyson, and Maurizio Fava, the link between associations and mood in both healthy and depressed individuals.[2] (On a side note, what makes such studies difficult to execute is that for clearer findings, we need to recruit depressed individuals who are not medicated, or else the results will be contaminated by the medication and by the fact that the level of their depression might be modulated by varying degrees of treatment success. But once we find such individuals, our higher responsibility is to encourage them to seek treatment. Nevertheless, there are depressed individuals who are not on medications for a host of reasons, and those are the patients who participated in our experiment. It is illuminating that even when we recruit individuals randomly from the general population, we screen them formally and often enough find some who are clinically depressed, even if they did not know that themselves because they had not sought diagnosis before.) In our fMRI experiment, all participants viewed pictures of objects that are known to activate strong contextual associations, like a roulette wheel or a construction helmet, while their brains were scanned in MRI. As predicted, healthy individuals activated the cortical network of associations to a higher extent than the depressed individuals, supporting the notion that people with depression are less associative.

In addition, given that the degree of rumination is a continuum, we measured rumination level for each participant so that we can compare it with corresponding changes in the brain. Before turning to the findings, it is worth expanding about how ruminative thinking is exactly measured, given that this is such a debilitating phenomenon of thought. One standard questionnaire is called the Ruminative Responses

Scale, developed by the late pioneer Susan Nolen-Hoeksema and her colleagues.[3] Here it is in full:

RUMINATION SCALE

People think and do many different things when they feel depressed. Please read each of the items below and indicate whether you almost never, sometimes, often, or almost always think or do each one when you feel down, sad, or depressed. Please indicate what you generally do, not what you think you should do.

1 almost never 2 sometimes 3 often 4 almost always

1. think about how alone you feel
2. think "I won't be able to do my job if I don't snap out of this"
3. think about your feelings of fatigue and achiness
4. think about how hard it is to concentrate
5. think "What am I doing to deserve this?"
6. think about how passive and unmotivated you feel
7. analyze recent events to try to understand why you are depressed
8. think about how you don't seem to feel anything anymore
9. think "Why can't I get going?"
10. think "Why do I always react this way?"
11. go away by yourself and think about why you feel this way
12. write down what you are thinking about and analyze it
13. think about a recent situation, wishing it had gone better
14. think "I won't be able to concentrate if I keep feeling this way"
15. think "Why do I have problems other people don't have?"
16. think "Why can't I handle things better?"
17. think about how sad you feel
18. think about all your shortcomings, failings, faults, mistakes
19. think about how you don't feel up to doing anything
20. analyze your personality to try to understand why you are depressed
21. go someplace alone to think about your feelings
22. think about how angry you are with yourself

The rumination score of an individual is simply the sum of her numeric responses to all the questions above.

Our analysis showed that the neuronal volume of the hippocampus, a brain complex that is key for both memory and mood, was directly correlated with the extent of rumination. Within the subfields of the hippocampus, we found increased or decreased structural volume depending on the individual level of ruminative tendencies. It is worth noting that beyond neuronal cell bodies, the gray matter consists also of dendrites and axons, synapses, glial cells, and capillaries, so a change in volume can involve a change in more than one component. To put it simply, thinking style affects not only our mood but also the structure of our brains. It was already known that depression diminishes the volume of the hippocampus and that various therapies for mood disorder, such as selective serotonin reuptake inhibitors (SSRI, like Prozac), psychotherapy, aerobic exercise, and meditation can help regain hippocampal volume. But showing that this volume corresponds to how much we tend to ruminate solidifies the link between thinking and feeling.

For decades, depression has been taken as a disorder of chemical imbalance. Our approach shows that it is just as much a disorder of thought imbalance. There is a cascade of influence in the cortex. Medications aim to regulate the levels of neurotransmitters such as serotonin, and these levels then affect upward all the way to mood and thinking style. Our approach, as cognitive neuroscientists, is instead to address the top level, thought, with the hope that untangling ruminations will not only improve mood but also trickle down in that cascade to normalize levels of the neurotransmitters. A bidirectional cascade with multiple entry points will potentially alleviate the overall symptoms of mood disorders.

Our memory consists of a giant web of representations that are connected to each other with several degrees of separation (chair ➜ table ➜ wood ➜ forest ➜ hiking ➜ vacation ➜ relax ➜ piña colada). While this makes for an efficient framework for memory encoding and retrieval, we would not want our brain to activate the cortical representation of piña colada every time we see a chair. It is crucial that the activation of one mental representation would activate associated representations so that we can generate predictions about what to expect but in doing so activate only the associations that are relevant in the specific context and not beyond. To curb the extent of the representations that are activated simultaneously, the brain exerts inhibition like brakes. In normal levels of inhibition, our mind is still given the mental space to be sufficiently associative. In negative mood and in depression, however, there is excessive inhibition, and as a result the extent of associative activation is severely constrained. In other words, overinhibition diminishes our ability to disengage from cyclical thinking and debilitating rumination. Underinhibition, on the other hand, can cause hallucinations in its extreme because of activation of superfluous associations, as in schizophrenia. Inhibition has to be just right.

This link between breadth of mental activation and mood leads to some counterintuitive possibilities. For example, the thinking pattern of individuals with ADHD can be seen as the exact opposite of rumination, with both thought and attention widely spread (believe me, I know) and with reduced inhibition (hence the impulsive behavior but also creativity that are often associated with ADHD). The connection we have established between mental scope and mood suggests that ADHD would entail a better mood, and indeed there is evidence for elevated mood in ADHD. Unfortunately, this mood benefit is not stable because it is often offset by negative responses to the reduced ability to focus, such as frustration and irritability, and the mood benefit is thus often countered and the ultimate outcome is that ADHD is often accompanied by mood swings. Furthermore, medications designed to focus the

ADHD mind often result not only in improved concentration but also in a deteriorated mood.

Positive mood as reward for broad thinking might be nature's way of encouraging us to explore, learn, and be creative. Look long and wide for the new rather than exploit the familiar. I believe that you should think less to think better. But if you do think, think broader to feel better.

Creativity and Broad Mindwandering

Another unfortunate outcome of narrow and ruminative thinking is that our creativity is tamped down. The research showing this intersects with my work on associative thinking. Making novel associations is one of the key elements of creativity. The more preprogrammed our thinking is, the less likely innovative connections are to be made and fewer creative ideas will bubble up. We've found that the reverse is also true: that mindwandering can enhance creativity, that is, if the mindwandering is of the open, broadly associative type.

In one of our studies on the link between mindwandering and creativity, we differentially taxed people's cognitive capacity, and thus their ability to mindwander, by asking them to keep in mind either a long or a short string of digits while they were engaged in a free-association task.[4] Compare having to remember the string 6839503 with having to remember 47 throughout the experiment, while having to respond with a quick association for each word given to you. To make it even more authentic, the time allotted for their response was limited to be very brief. Imagine you have half a second to say the first thing that comes to mind when you hear the word "shoe" or "mother" or "potato." It is challenging, but sure to provide entertainment to you and those around you; you would be surprised. The longer string poses a higher "cognitive load," which we found to be directly affecting the originality of the responses. Those participants with a lower load (short string) provided more creative and more remote associations, while those with the higher load (long string) provided the most mundane responses. It can be manifested in pretty simple terms. For example, the word "white" will result in the more common association "black" by a participant who had to keep in mind the long string, and the more original response "yogurt" from a participant who needed to remember only a two-digit string. It is easy to see how this translates to real-world situations, with real-world stressors that load our mind and take away from our ability to be our creative selves.

Using the simple but potent task of "thought sampling," we were also able to demonstrate the link between mindwandering and creativity more extensively, discovering that during a state of increased creativity, people's thinking is broadly associative. In a complementary line of studies, published in the *Proceedings of the National Academy of Sciences*, we increased levels of mindwandering using external electrical stimulation to the prefrontal cortex through the skull (transcranial direct current stimulation, or tDCS). We found that with increased mindwandering came improved cognitive performance as well.[5] That we managed to influence mindwandering with external electrical stimulation is another novel and surprising aspect of that study.

Our Curious Need to Create

We take for granted even the most amazing things. One such thing dawned on me just the other day: I can lie down on my sofa with my laptop and watch pretty much any movie that was ever made, read any book that was ever published, and listen to any song that was ever recorded.

As a kid, growing up in Dimona in the South of Israel, I had to wait for Pink Floyd's *The Wall* for almost six months after its release. A new movie would take three months to reach Israel from Hollywood, and it would then play for a couple of weeks straight as the only movie in town. Now this whole world is on my sofa, in an instant. Why not spend my entire life absorbing all this goodness then?

Assuming you have enough food in your fridge and a roof over your head, what stops you from just being lost in what the modern world can offer for your eternal pleasure is your inherent need to do and create. We are curious creatures, sure, thirsty for knowledge in all domains conceivable, but just as compulsive is our need to use this knowledge to create. We choose not to disappear into fantasy, sensual poetry, and moving melodies even if we could, because we prefer to do instead.

By creativity I do not mean necessarily inventing a flying cab. Most of what we do regularly involves some creation or production: from making food to fixing a leaky shower, from writing a letter to gardening. And so, even thinking is an act of creation. New ideas, new inventions, new plans you make while your mind wanders are all products that your mind created. Practicing Jews observe the Shabbat, which includes the restriction of not creating. You cannot paint, write, build, or generate anything new during this holy day. When I want to give my religious friends a hard time, I tell them that their mind continues to generate new knowledge even when they just sit around the dinner table. All those mental simulations our minds are constantly engaged in result in new connections inside the cortex. Those imagined experiences that remain in memory are sheer acts of creation.

In numerous domains of our existence, it seems that we humans need to be on the move. We can't sit still for long, we cannot focus on the same theme for an extended duration, and even our eyes move all the time (even when we think we are fixated on one spot, our eyes still perform constant little movements that are called microsaccades). Similarly, our mind does not pause and needs to move forward almost compulsively by creating more and more new and useful things such as thoughts, objects, and actions. Creation is movement, which is vital for our well-being.

Improving Mood Through Creative, Associative Thinking

The proposition that the sheer scope of thought might affect mood was initially provocative, given the prevailing emphasis at the time on the chemical correlates of depression in the brain. But as I delved further into the broader literature on mood, I made an exciting discovery. A group of researchers, chief among them Alice Isen at Cornell University, had already demonstrated the other direction of the link we have proposed: they showed that better mood is correlated with broad thinking. This was so thrilling to me that I vividly remember the moment I read her description of the finding.

Such is the beauty of scientific endeavor. You generate a long-shot hypothesis that is based on crumbs and on your own imagination, you turn to the literature, and sometimes you find just the perfect piece of the puzzle you need to proceed on the right path. Now what remained for me to do was to test whether the reverse also works and broadening thinking will improve mood. The idea is that thinking style that is broadly associative prevents rumination by "distracting" the thought process away from dwelling on a narrow, negative theme, and it affords the expansive mental motion required for moving on with our lives. I immediately began conducting studies in which we assisted people in getting into a broadly associative state of mind and assessed the effect on their mood. And sure enough, they were feeling happier.[6]

How did we help people get into that frame of mind? It may sound overly simplistic, but it was done by merely having people read associative lists of individual words that advance broadly. Reading lists that expanded associatively in a progressive manner, such as orange–juice–Campari–Italy–vacation–ski–snow–cold improved mood significantly compared with reading associative lists of words that were designed to emulate ruminative thinking by advancing much more narrowly, such as dinner–plate–fork–knife–spoon–table–tablecloth–napkin, or by chains of words that were not directly associated with each other, such as cow–newspaper–strawberry–pencil–watch–light–airplane–donut. I know these chains are fun to read and are highly informative, so here are a few more examples of corresponding broad and narrow associative lists:

BROAD ASSOCIATIONS

1. yarn–sweater–winter–snow–ice–skate–speed–race–car–horn–band–drums
2. dog–bone–chicken–rooster–farm–cow–milk–cookies–chocolate–cake–birthday–candles
3. worm–apple–orange–juice–coffee–tea–milk–cookies–bake–oven–microwave–popcorn
4. thread–needle–shot–nurse–doctor–drugs–alcohol–beer–wine–cheese–mouse–trap
5. wolf–moon–star–telescope–microscope–flask–whiskey–Scotland–sheep–cow–barn–farmer
6. wine–bottle–coke–root-beer–ice–cream–cherry–pie–apple–seed–plant–leaves–rake
7. whale–dolphin–tuna–sushi–rice–paper–pencil–typewriter–manuscript–book–glasses–eyes

NARROW ASSOCIATIONS

1. yarn–knit–thread–sew–wool–string–crochet–weave–needle–spool–sweater–ball
2. dog–cat–puppy–animal–friend–house–food–biscuit–pet–collar–bone–pound
3. worm–earth–fishing–wiggle–crawl–dirt–ground–bird–slimy–apple–bait–hole
4. thread–needle–sew–string–cloth–clothes–rope–thimble–sewing–machine–pin–spool–yarn
5. wolf–animal–dog–gang–fox–teeth–bear–moon–howl–danger–woods–cat
6. wine–beer–red–cellar–cheese–grape–dinner–glass–drunk–white–alcohol–bottle
7. whale–fish–big–blubber–ocean–mammal–shark–dolphin–large–save–water–killer

Another surprisingly simple method for improving mood in the lab is by making participants read text exceptionally rapidly.[7] In this study, one letter was presented at a time, from a statement, starting at two hundred milliseconds per letter gradually down to forty milliseconds per letter, and this resulted in markedly improved mood. Interestingly, this beneficial effect of reading speed on mood is obtained regardless of whether the text contains positive or negative content. Even text designed to depress mood elevated mood when being read rapidly. The explanation is that reading fast induces a manic-like state, which is known to be accompanied by elation. Indeed, after reading fast, participants showed other characteristics of mania, such as a subjective feeling of power, creativity, a sense of increased energy, and exaggerated self-esteem.

The mood improvements reported above were all demonstrated on healthy individuals. We are currently trying these cognitive methods with individuals diagnosed with depression. Depression, of course, has various flavors, magnitudes, and patterns of responsiveness to different therapeutic approaches. But at least for those whose symptoms are governed by a strong ruminative element, we suspect that using cognitive exercises to broaden associative thinking will help rebuild the cortical infrastructure in a way that will allow them to recover the healthy associative thinking style. Simply put, rumination causes structural losses in the brain, and practicing the opposite, broad thinking, could help regain that lost volume and along the way elevate mood.

One of the most exciting discoveries in neuroscience research in recent decades is *adult neurogenesis*: the growth of new neurons even at older ages.[8] This discovery sparked a wave of optimism. We continue to grow; it is not only about cell death and declining with age, but new brain cells can be born throughout life. Like in many big discoveries, the details are still somewhat murky, and there is no lack of debate surrounding it, but still it is groundbreaking. Neurogenesis is limited to two regions of the brain: one is the olfactory bulb, which is not relevant here and hasn't been studied much yet, and the other is in the hippocampus, specifically in a subfield within the hippocampus called the dentate gyrus. Depression reduces the volume of the hippocampus, at least partially because it hurts the capacity for neurogenesis. On the upside, increasing neurogenesis helps alleviate depression and anxiety symptoms.[9] Furthermore, successful pharmacological (medication) and psychotherapy treatments, as well as running, have been shown to increase neurogenesis.[10] Finally, blocking hippocampal neurogenesis from taking place reduces the effectiveness of antidepressants. It is not clear yet how these newborn neurons integrate and assimilate into existing neural circuits, and how exactly they alleviate depression symptoms, but generalization and broader thinking are possible venues to explore. Because the hippocampus is central both for mood and for memory, adult neurogenesis provides hope not only for depression but also for dementia and Alzheimer's disease.[11] We believe that our approach capitalizes on the same mechanism, helping individuals with depression regain proper neurogenesis by renewing their ability for broad associative mindwandering. Mindwandering, then, the broadly associative type, not only can help us learn from our imagined experience, and help us in improving our mood, but can also change our brain.

The good news for most of us about getting into an associative frame of mind is that it actually comes naturally, if we let it. We've all had some experience with this uplifting mindwandering—through daydreaming. In fact, that the experience of daydreaming is enjoyable is a defining part of the experience. The earliest definition of daydreaming, from the 1680s, is "a reverie, pleasant and visionary fancy indulged in when awake."[12] So, here again, while we tend to think of daydreaming as wasting time, there's good reason our minds are given to it. It's all the more reason that we should all allow ourselves to engage in it sometimes, maybe even make it part of our daily or weekly routine. In fact, we can even combine intentional mindwandering with other activities. Before I go on a run, or to the supermarket, I like to erase what's just been occupying my mind, especially if it was something like the bills I just paid or an annoying email. I wipe it away by replacing it with some engaging reading, such as a few pages from an Aldous Huxley book. Or if I want to stimulate creative thinking about a paper I'm working on, I'll read some of that. Then when I'm running, my mindwandering will tend to mull over what I just read. This is a way of intentionally inducing the cognitive process called "incubation," which is what leads to the aha! moments we've all had, where ideas seem to just pop up out of nowhere. That said, we will do right to think of our mindwandering stream as having a mind of its own; by the definition of those wild wanderings, we cannot dictate their direction. If they were not so unpredictable and uncontrollable, they would not be so beneficial for us in generating creative solutions for life's events. But replacing the content of our working memory with stuff that we would like to develop further while we wander brings us closer.

Learning about the links between broadly associative mindwandering, creativity, and mood was the key for me in combining all that I had learned about our default thinking into the new overall understanding of our exploratory-versus-exploitatory thinking modes. The route there passed through my dive into silence.

CHAPTER TEN

MEDITATION, THE DEFAULT BRAIN, AND THE QUALITY OF OUR EXPERIENCE

FOR MY FIFTIETH BIRTHDAY, I DECIDED TO GIVE A TRY TO SOME MINDFULness training. I'd been quite skeptical from the little I'd tried and read about meditation, but I was intrigued by a spate of recent findings in neuroscience about its positive effects, from improved memory and attention to increased creativity and reduced stress. In fact, even as little as an eight-week mindfulness course is sufficient to show marked increases in gray-matter density in multiple brain structures, including the hippocampus and the prefrontal cortex.[1] I had just moved back to Israel, and I heard from a good friend, also a neuroscientist, that she was attending a weeklong Vipassana meditation retreat. ("Vipassana" means insight, or "tovana" in Hebrew, which was also the name of the organization running the retreat.) It required unplugging from all electronics and complete silence all week, and though I doubted I'd be able to keep strictly to the silence, the notion of escaping for a while all cell phone chirping, email pinging, and screen staring had huge appeal. So there I found myself, on a kibbutz, with sixty Israelis in search of inner peace, sitting in an old Bauhaus building designed by architects who fled the Nazis, listening to the soft voice of a deep-blue-eyed British guru, overshadowed periodically by the prayer of the imam coming from a neighboring Arab village. What amazing juxtapositions life can summon.

Waking up and going to sleep at hours that were foreign to me (5:00 a.m. and 9:30 p.m., respectively), eating vegan, sleeping in bunk beds, and sharing a room with three hairy strangers, with one set of bathroom facilities at the end of the corridor—what could be better! We endured hourlong sessions of silent sitting, silent standing, silent (and excruciatingly slow) walking, and silent lying.

I hated it at first. But in that one week of silence, I learned more about thinking in general, and about my own thinking in particular, than I had in years as a brain scientist. How absurd, I thought, when our instructor told us to "observe" our thoughts. I gave it a try, and I quickly learned to view my thoughts. Playing along and changing perspectives is all it took.

Once you start attending your thoughts, though, you quickly understand you are in serious trouble. They race, they intrude, they stick, they bother, and they grow and grow. So the next skill to learn is to help those thoughts move along, turn them into visitors rather than permanent residents of your mental and emotional work space. Initially, I found the attempt to simply let those thoughts go impossible. I seemed to be achieving the opposite effect. Either thoughts whirled through my mind like the proverbial bat out of hell, or I slipped into rumination and became anxious. Thankfully, the friend of mine attending had agreed to cheat about the silence during nightly walks, so I could ask her questions about the experience. I didn't feel guilty; I had come to learn, and she knew a great deal about the strange practice. When I complained to her about how unpleasant my attempts at chaperoning my thoughts were, she told me about labeling. What a revelation.

Manipulating Thoughts

Thoughts can have a direct influence on our well-being. In particular, a bothering thought can be really disruptive, and in some cases stopping that thought is all we want. Extreme cases give rise to desperate behavior. Take self-harming as an example. Individuals suffering from mood disorders such as post-trauma, depression, and anxiety, as well as a host of other mental disorders, suffer so much from intrusive thoughts that they can resort to self-mutilation. The idea that one would prefer the physical pain of cutting her own arm with a knife over the mental pain of a bothering thought is hard to fathom.

Research in cognitive psychology, combined with experience with psychotherapy and the practice of meditation, teaches us very clearly that we cannot get rid of thoughts just by wishing. In fact, if we try to stop thinking of something specific deliberately, we curiously achieve the exact opposite effect; we think about this very same topic obsessively. As Fyodor Dostoyevsky said in *Winter Notes on Summer Impressions*, "Try to pose for yourself this task: not to think of a polar bear, and you will see that the cursed thing will come to mind every minute." This intuition was later supported by beautiful research, pioneered by the late Dan Wegner, with the phenomenon that was later dubbed "the ironic process." Trying to stop a thought is not some fancy experimental task reserved for a lab setting but rather an everyday necessity for all of us. From suppression of thoughts and feelings, as has been described by Freud and others, to trying to avoid thinking about various traumas, and trying to stay in control by not worrying too much, not thinking is a constant challenge. Without our ability not to think about certain things, we would not be able to board an airplane, eat meat (I don't), or forgive.

Here, again, my silence retreats taught me things I did not know. There are two efficient ways to make a thought disappear. The first is to acknowledge the thought and face it head-on, like is done also in psychological therapy. The second is to acknowledge it and then give that thought a label, or a name, which would usually put it in a mental "box" so it stops reappearing involuntarily. (Note that the term "labeling" is also mentioned earlier when we talk about how we give familiar objects around us names, labels, and thus often miss the rich details, not to be confused with thought labeling as described here.)

With these newfound understandings, I started playing and experimenting. How do acknowledging and labeling work? You examine a specific thought that occupies your mind and label it along a couple of dimensions. Is it positive, negative, or neutral in terms of the emotions that it elicits? Is it about the past, present, or future? Is it about you, others, or both? So, if you think about a compliment you received last week from someone important to you, this thought will be labeled as: positive, past, self. If you worry about the puppy you gave for adoption to someone whose attitude toward animals you were not sure about, this thought will be labeled as: negative, future, others. You engage in this exercise, and thoughts start to disappear as soon as you finish labeling them. At some point, I started to imagine hearing that swoosh sound of an email being sent off. I started to feel in control. So what if worries float into your mind? You acknowledge them, stick a label on them, and move on to new arising thoughts.

This simple approach was already enough to achieve some sort of inner silence, much less of a hustling-and-bustling racing mind. When I ran out, I tried to force a new thought, to deliberately think about that thing I wanted to achieve at work, or the financial future of my children, but new chatty thoughts would not develop. And then strange, sometimes amazing, usually pleasurable things start to happen to you. The result of this process, at least it was for me on a handful of lucky occasions, is an eerily empty mind. Nothing is happening inside, an experience guaranteed to feel strange and awesome at the same time. (For a scary moment, I started to worry that my mind would stay empty and I would not be able to get back to work after the retreat . . .) And with this inner silence came stunning new sensations, with amplified resolution. I vividly felt soft wind moving the little hairs on my arm or a ray of sun on my face, and the mundane touch of a fork on my lips felt almost erotic. It was sensory poetry afforded by an unoccupied mind.

Such magical experiences, however, are few and far between. I took those occasional states as welcomed side effects. I really was there to learn what meditation practice does to my thoughts and experience, so reaching a state close to emptiness was fascinating enough for me, independent of any intense bodily sensations that may or may not accompany the practice.

Next on my curiosity-driven agenda was to try to bring back thoughts I had already labeled and sent into oblivion back to the foreground. Interestingly, I could not. It was as if they have been sealed, locked, or evaporated (or simply stored deep in my memory). Pause to ponder this for a moment: a nagging thought, worry, obsession, or fear that you could not rid yourself of, no matter how hard you tried, not only efficiently disappears merely by attaching a label to it, but you can hardly bring it back even if you wanted. (Of course, some thoughts, like intrusive memories from a trauma, or persistent ruminations, need a heavier artillery than just thought labeling.) This revelation was amazing in how powerful and novel it felt, and it had opened for me a door toward a better understanding of mind, feelings, and experience.

You might have noticed how the moment you decide to write a reminder to yourself on a note, that something you need to remember so badly vanishes from your conscious mind (or working memory, more precisely). You stop clinging to it once you have put it in writing. You have delegated your foreground mental processing to the little note. This is similar to what happens to a labeled thought as it disappears.

We suffer from (or enjoy) thoughts less when they have been labeled because they are then encapsulated. A word simplifies the way we handle complicated thoughts and concepts. If I tell you about someone who is not physically stable, does not speak coherently, smells bad, and his behavior is overall inappropriate, you will be worried and unsure how to approach him if you need to. But if I say only one word about him, "drunk," everything is clear and manageable in an instant. It is like when a doctor gives a diagnosis after hearing a list of symptoms; we give a label to describe a thought or a concept. And what happens to feelings that cannot be put into a label because they are too abstract? We use those categorical dimensions of positive or negative, self or others, past, present, or future, and so on, and it forces just anything to be labeled. It is a method for tricking the amorphous.

Take as another example the question of why talking about my "issues" makes them less of an issue. The mere utterance of a concerning thought, like acknowledging it aloud, can improve feelings markedly. At some point I started to believe that I could talk to a wall, as long as I talked concretely and explicitly, and it would be sufficient to bring about improvement. Indeed, I later learned that as suffering individuals put bothersome thoughts in writing, their symptoms are typically alleviated, even if they end up tearing that note apart without showing the note to anyone. Such "writing therapy" has even been claimed to help reduce the effects of trauma. Just acknowledging to oneself, explicitly and specifically, seems to suffice.[2]

Marion Milner, in *A Life of One's Own*, writes eloquently about similar individual revelations, how merely admitting thoughts makes them less of a bother. In one such example, she describes sitting on the grass on a summer day, which felt instead like a foggy November day to her at that instance, in Cornwall, trying to put into words what worried her. She found out that it was a previous encounter with a man to whom she had felt attracted, and that attraction had not materialized. She realized that she had been going over and over that encounter, what we call ruminations in the context of depression and other mood disorders. But then just talking to herself intentionally about the incident and what worried her about it made those ruminations less obsessive. Admitting thoughts—confessing, acknowledging, accepting—is akin to labeling by attaching names to thoughts, and it makes them vanish.

Interestingly, the same principle works for physical sensations, not just mental events and worries. You feel a fly on your arm (and they seem to land on you more often when you meditate and are trying to sit still . . .), and your first reaction is to try to scare it away, just like when you are trying to remove a thought by actively aiming to get rid of it. It disrupts, it is intrusive, and it is inefficient. Simply give in and let whatever it is be—a thought or an itch; look at them and acknowledge rather than try to push them away, and they seem to find their place. Don't will it; allow it. I have to admit that talk such as this, about acknowledging thoughts and allowing things, used to seem to me unbearably abstract and unsubstantiated. But it works, and as a brain scientist and as a human this fascinates me. Admitting thoughts helps us label thoughts, thereby facilitating their detachment and propagation away from the front stage of our thinking.

This concept of relief through explicit expression is reminiscent of the concept of catharsis, especially in the context of psychological therapy. Either via the (scientifically somewhat debatable) method of hypnosis or with the method of free associations, a patient is encouraged to express inner thoughts aloud. This method allows patients to describe feelings and memories associated with a certain event from their past that have not been addressed properly before. Much of the alleviation associated with such psychotherapeutical treatment has been attributed to the "purifying" feeling of catharsis. Explanations as to why sharing would bring relief range from a presumed sense of closure to that of reduced ambiguity, to which we know humans are averse. But these are not formal scientific accounts just yet. For now, it is interesting to consider the possibility that disturbing thoughts are a result of unsettled or distorted memories. This is especially pronounced in the context of trauma.

Victims who suffer from intrusive thoughts and memories, nightmares, and depression can find relief in such a method that encourages revisiting the details of the trauma in a way that seems to promote a proper reconsolidation of the original memories. It is as if a traumatic event becomes a source of haunting memories because it has not been consolidated properly at the time when it happened. Possibly it is because of heightened arousal and intense emotions, because of selective attention to some details but not others, or some active suppression of certain aspects. (A less known fact about memory is that we first consolidate a new memory so it remains stored in a stable manner, but each time we retrieve this memory is an opportunity, voluntary or not, for this memory to be reshaped by new contextual information, and then this memory is reconsolidated in an updated form. This is valuable for enriched learning as well as for correcting distortions from the original consolidation.) It could be in an exposure therapy where patients are asked to recall the events and details of the trauma while focusing on the "hot spots," the most disturbing aspects of the memory, or it could be in treatments involving drugs that release inhibitions, thereby allowing traumatized patients to revisit the source of their trauma more readily and in a more homogenous manner.

Disturbing thoughts are not unique to trauma and are actually very familiar to all of us on a daily basis. We always worry about something, either consciously or not. Sharing these concerns with someone, a friend or a therapist, or admitting and labeling that disturbing thought has a similar effect to that of the exposure therapy in trauma described above. To share honestly, or to label, you are forced to activate all aspects and consider them evenly: pleasant, neutral, or unpleasant; past, present, or future; self or others; inward oriented or outward oriented; verbal or visual. We label thoughts, and we label emotions. This separates a feeling from a thought, and then the feeling becomes clearer and the thought less dominant. Sharing or labeling puts things in proper perspective, and poof, the thought, and the intense emotions associated with it, is gone. It is stored neatly with no need to call for your inner attention by continuing to intrude on you. Haunting memories may be our subconscious's way of calling for proper consideration and a more balanced reconsolidation, as psychoanalysis also suggests. If so, then intrusive memories have an adaptive value, regardless of how we feel about them.

Secret Thoughts

We all know someone who simply cannot keep a secret. The one I know, Aunt Roniti, will tell you what she has heard, regardless of whether it is a secret. The only difference is that before she divulges a secret, she will first whisper, "But this is secret." In fact, as Freud concluded, no mortal can keep a secret.

Many believe that our inability to contain a secret, while still forced not to speak about it explicitly, makes our brain and body find other ways to express it on our behalf. Even as little as fidgeting with an object might be our body's way of telling our secret to the world. In the eighties Japanese movie *A Taxing Lady*, two tax investigators for the Japanese National Tax Agency go to interview a master of tax evasion. Before going into his studio, the senior investigator tells his assistant that he is going to ask the con where his safe is, and the assistant's role is to watch closely the suspect's eyes and see where he looks immediately as the question is asked. The assistant has to look closely because the suspect is going to move his gaze to the location of that safe ever so quickly before moving his eyes back to the investigator and saying he has no safe. And this is exactly what happened. This is a movie, of course, not science. And even the fact that I have tried this trick several times myself, like getting the location of some software disks I really wanted from a secretary who was hiding them from me, does not make it science. But science does support this notion of truth-telling bodies, hands in particular.[3]

A lot has already been said about secrets, but not enough about the mental and physical toll they take. Some of us have already noticed individually that secrets require constant effort. Beyond guilt and other social discomfort, they simply represent a load on our mental and emotional reserves. Keeping secrets, especially charged ones, has been reported to cause all kinds of physical ailments (from cold to chronic disease) as well as mental disturbances (depression). I once knew an older lady who was lively and optimistic as well as a cancer survivor. She was convinced, as she told me, that her cancer was a result of hiding her affair with her future husband from her then present husband. This is not the first time I heard such individual and informal reports, which align well with scientific reports on the possibly devastating effects of secrets or guilt on health.[4] Of course, some secrets are better kept as secrets in that their knowledge might cause more harm, so this is not a categorical statement.

There are voluntary secrets that we deliberately choose to hide, and there is suppression of disturbing things we do not want to think about; there are secrets we hide from others and secrets we hide from ourselves. They all make us suffer to some extent. They are all a burden on our mental capacities, and all for the same reason. That reason has to do with inhibition in the brain. Refraining from saying (or doing) something is not a passive operation but rather an active one, which requires metabolic and mental energy. When it is sustained for longer durations, it depletes our ability to fully process percepts, emotions, and our inner and outer environments.

The possible negative effects of keeping secrets are intriguing but less relevant for our business here. More interesting for us is the benefits of being open and of sharing. Sharing a secret, as Aunt Roniti knows best, alleviates and relieves. Not talking, suppressing: all involve applying costly inhibition. On the other hand, talking and expressing free precious mental resources for more worthy activities such as creative ideation. Indeed, reduced inhibition could improve mood both because releasing inhibition triggers the release of endorphins, those fun molecules, and because freeing resources makes us more creative, which is also tied to better mood here. That said, some inhibition is mandatory when living in a society, which is what stops you from touching an attractive random person at a restaurant, for example, and also should have stopped me from saying what I just did . . .

You can see by now the link being made here between how we handle thoughts in meditation, how it is akin to sharing, and how one may expect the same benefits as when sharing inner thoughts with others. Sharing, in meditation, is really just with yourself, acknowledging, to the fullest, with no need for an outside listener.

By teaching you to clean up your mind from stray thoughts, meditation helps you get better at appreciating the rich details of life. You become more acutely observant of the present moment, the sights and sounds, the sensation elicited by a breeze, the taste of a fresh strawberry.

How Meditation Makes Us Mindful: A Neuroscientist's Perspective

You sit down on a pillow, observe your thoughts, and keep coming back to focus on your breath in great detail; how is this turning you to be mindful? There are three components that I see as a scientist and a part-time practitioner that can explain the power of meditation to foster mindful life. The first is *diffused attention*: the ability to attend your environment with equal weight to all locations and all items surrounding you, with no bias and no privileged allocation. It's akin to what Freud called "evenly hovering attention," which he recommended psychoanalysts to adopt as a means for remaining open to new observations. We all should. Usually, attention means the exact opposite: focusing on a very specific and typically narrow location or feature, and ignoring, even suppressing, everything that falls outside that attention "spotlight." But it is claimed, and for many already proven, that the practice of meditation allows you to take your entire environment as equally important and of potential interest. When there is no top-down guidance of what or where to orient your attention, your attention is oriented nowhere and everywhere.

The second thing that meditation does to your brain to make it mindful is to turn off expectations. The default state of our brain is to expect: to expect something to happen, to expect something to be good or bad, to want something in the future, and to judge things in comparison with our anticipation. Watching your ongoing breath is the head fake that makes you be here and now. And by being here and now, you are cut off from thinking about the future, which is what expectation is all about. When you expect nothing, you are open to whatever is coming.

The third component that makes meditation so effective for the quality of present experience is reducing clinging to our thoughts, desires, and fears. The main element in constricting the breadth of our thought, and the flow of our ideas, is inhibition. Inhibition is the force that limits the span of thought, of associative activation, and the progression of our mental movement as a whole: speed, scope, and distance. A more inhibited person will more likely suffer from mood disorders, while a less inhibited person will be more creative, to put it somewhat simplistically. In meditation, this translates into whether one tends to cling to a thought or instead lets it flow. When there is less inhibition, there is less stagnation and more progression.

There is a major mechanistic link that ties together these three factors that are required for mindfulness, which is how much influence is granted for top-down processes. This is to be compared with how much weight is given to the bottom-up processes. As I will describe in detail in the last chapter, what determines our state of mind is the relative emphasis given to top-down compared with bottom-up signals, how much our overall state incorporates information arriving from memory compared with how much from the senses. This ratio dictates our mood, the associative breadth of our thoughts, and the scope of our attention and perception. All three items above are shaped by top-down processing. Attentional guidance is determined from the top down, and diffused attention means zero top-down guidance of attention: all is equal, no spotlight. Turning off expectations—that's the second one—also implies turning off top-down signals, those that normally send down predictions and knowledge from memory to be compared with the input. Last, inhibition is also of a top-down origin, which is a major concern in depression and a cause for rumination. Letting go of thoughts is directly related to reduced top-down commands: less top-down ➤ less inhibition ➤ less being stuck ➤ more progression.

In sum, although top-down influences are critically helpful in numerous circumstances, as we have seen, in the present context top-down processes can have three types of negative effects on our state of mind and thought: constricting attentional focus, sending down memory-based expectations, and dictating the extent of inhibition. All three are modulated by mindfulness meditation.

These are not the exact same top-down mechanisms in all three influences. Attentional guidance, predictive signals, and inhibition are all top-down forces in the brain but with different anatomical origins, an overlapping but not identical involvement of various neurotransmitters, different timelines of influence, and so on. What they have in common, though, is that they all represent forms of internal top-down control of how we experience things in our world: either locally, with anticipation and with limited scope, or globally, tabula rasa, with fewer constraints.

Naturally, it is not meant that yogis sit and explicitly aim at their prefrontal cortex to reduce top-down influences; most people do not even know where the prefrontal cortex is, and even then cortical activation is generally not subjected to our conscious control. The operation is more reminiscent of neurofeedback techniques, where the individual and the practice reinforce and strengthen what works well. By following the guidelines of meditation practice, one influences these top-down sources without thinking of them as such. You focus on your breath, and you do not cling to thoughts, over and over; you repeat and reinforce the practices that, unbeknownst to you, diminish the effects of top-down impositions, and it just works. Obviously, the ancient practice of meditation was not developed by taking into account all these recent neuroscience findings and knowledge. Instead, the practice was developed to optimize presence and quality of experience, and it just so happened that the major pillars of this tried practice are all related to diminishing the role of top-down influences, in all of its different flavors, in our lives.

Being mindful of our thoughts, and more generally of our inner working, also transcends to being mindful of our environment. Gradually, you notice that less irrelevant thoughts pop up, and you are more and more free to experience life, and the only ingredient that remains to be added for rich, aware living is immersion. Once we have found our present, the next move is to step in.

If I had to sit down and write my entire life so far, every detail I can recall, it would be a 250-page book, if that. Fifty-five years, about twenty thousand days, that's almost a half-million hours of things happening to me or by me, and all I can remember can be put in a single book. I have often wondered where my third grade vanished to, for example, or my middle two years in engineering school, or the many family dinners I had as a child, or as a parent, and I feel I have been robbed. And the robber was me. Not being mindful, not being here and now, not really participating, is not being present in your life. How could I remember things I have not really witnessed and in which I did not really participate? I was there, but not really.

It seems that when you are mindful and immersed, the speed of the event you are experiencing slows down and the richness of the details is magnified manyfold. Soccer goalies during penalty kicks can see and respond to balls that are simply too fast for the rest of us even to perceive. They are super mindful, at least at those moments when the ball approaches them. I once drove an all-terrain vehicle (ATV) in the woods of Maine, with Nadia, my daughter, on my lap. I got too excited, and in one quick turn we rolled over. I still remember vividly the chain of events, as well as the chain of thoughts, with exceptional detail. I remember I was afraid she would be crushed by the heavy vehicle and how in what seemed like slow motion I lifted her and threw her to the side safely so that the ATV would miss her. The strength of the emotions made me exceptionally attentive and vigilant. Extreme circumstances call for your entire attentional resources. These are obviously not special powers that are reserved for extreme cases or for gifted goalies or baseball batters. This is merely your entire attention allocated toward one thing, in the now. Full attention is the trick.

The experience need not be so strong and consuming as a penalty kick to result in a mindful experience. If you were not distracted by irrelevant thoughts and inner chatter at all, this is how your perception could have been moment by moment, all day long, like Neo from *The Matrix*. Every event with your full participation would have been perceived and remembered like exciting novelty.

We all notice how time seems to pass faster as we age ("Jeez, is it New Year's again already?"). I used to think that this is because novelty makes us cherish moments for longer, and because there is less and less novelty as the world becomes more and more familiar to us, there are fewer opportunities for us to dwell and subjectively stretch time. But the key is attention. If we attend the moment, time prolongs, and if we manage to attend also the familiar afresh, we could make our time here feel longer—increasing our subjective longevity.

The Mindfulness Dilemma

Because meditation affects mindwandering at its core, it also influences the DMN. Numerous studies have shown this relationship by now. In one example, activity in the DMN was compared between experienced meditators and naive participants who just started while they performed different types of meditation ("Concentration," "Loving-Kindness," "Choiceless Awareness").[5] Activity in the default network was significantly lower in experienced meditators, which fits the many observations indicating that meditation diminishes the extent of mindwandering. In addition, connectivity between the different regions that make up the DMN was stronger for experienced meditators compared with the naive, implying that meditation also improves the efficiency of the communication between the different parts of the DMN. (This is a good place to emphasize a critical caveat when examining scientific findings, which we usually refer to as "Correlation does not imply causation." For example, here, it could be that the improved connectivity in meditators is an inherent characteristic of those who turn to and persist with meditation, not a property caused by meditation practice per se. That said, there are sufficient reports to support the notion that meditation indeed causes these effects, especially when monitoring individuals as they gain increasing experience with meditation.) Other research, pioneered by Richard Davidson at the University of Wisconsin–Madison, shows the positive effects of meditation on the regulation of emotions and on mental resilience.[6] More recently, meditation was also shown to improve attention and memory and to promote well-being and mental health in aging.[7] Clearly, meditation is good for you.

Meditation also makes room for experience. A new experience requires new brain activity and the availability of cortical resources. The busier is our brain at a given moment, the less we have available to allocate for a new experience. The new experience has to "elbow" its way in, and if our mind is already occupied, the resources left will allow for only a partial and superficial experience, if at all. Less of the sensations, associations, and emotions will be evoked with an occupied mind; the color red will not be as bright, and the flower will not be as beautiful. (Indeed, cognitive load also diminishes our ability to appreciate aesthetic beauty as well as our ability to feel pleasure. You can already see the link I am making between the cognitive load that constant ruminations impose on the depressed mind and the reduced ability to feel pleasure in depression, called anhedonia.) Therefore, it is clear that for quality of experience, we need fewer ongoing thoughts and more space for upcoming experiences to unfold with their full splendor in our brain. Meditation makes room for fresh experiences in its efficient way of dealing with ongoing and emerging thoughts. Thoughts come and go, and gradually you have less and less on your mind, and the next experience you attend is experienced much more fully, in higher resolution, mindfully. Mind fullness is the enemy of mindfulness.

But here comes the mindfulness dilemma. The better you get at exercising control over your thoughts and keeping your attention focused on the present moment, a funny—well, odd—thing happens. You start to observe yourself experiencing. You become not only more mindful of your experience, but also more mindful of yourself experiencing. You find yourself thinking, "I am listening to him, but I wonder if he can tell I am not following"; "They all respond so automatically, but not me"; "I am so famished. I hope nobody notices I'm eating like a pig"; "I'm so happy now that all my kids are around the table together and we are laughing." You are wonderfully mindful, you can appreciate the moment, and you pay attention to the center and the periphery of your field of vision, the foreground and the background of your present experience. You can observe your exaggerated reaction to a joke from a superior and instruct yourself not to suck up so blatantly. You can observe your irritation starting to flare up when someone is rude to you and neutralize it. This is good in many ways; you can reap great benefits from your increased monitoring of what is happening to you. But being attentive and mindful gradually changes our perspective on our experiences. We become witnesses, bystanders, rather than being the main characters in our very own life episodes.

Say that I've paid a large amount of money for the opportunity to drive a Formula 1 car for a couple of laps. I do not want to be observing myself driving. I want to be completely immersed in the experience: the thrill of the speed, the noise, the danger, and the smell of gasoline and burned tires; I want to be **in** my Formula 1 experience. Now that is fun. To be deeply immersed in an experience, so that all of your senses are alive and any worries vanish, with even the sense of self receded, is one of the greatest pleasures of life. So, while mindfulness training is of great value, and I highly recommend devoting regular time to it in our quest to optimize our present, we need to be aware of the downside of being just mindful and be open and ready to give up that perspective and immerse in our experiences. Don't be the dancer; be the dance.

CHAPTER ELEVEN

IMMERSED LIVING

NOT LONG AGO, AS I WAS HEADING OUT TO WORK, I APPROACHED MY young daughter Nili while she was having her breakfast. She was staring out of our big picture window, which looks out on a peaceful setting of leafy trees, and I figured she must be daydreaming. I asked her, "What are you thinking about, Nili?" "Nothing," she said. "I'm just looking outside," her tone conveying that she found the question odd. I could almost hear her exclaim in her mind, "Why should I be thinking about something?!" How wonderful to be so free of pesky mental preoccupations.

When was the last time you just sat and looked out a window without your mind flitting to something other than what you were observing, maybe the work you're backed up with, the flattering comment your spouse made the other day about your new shoes, or the time you were ten and your toy gun was stolen by bullies? Our thoughts can whisk us away in a blink to anywhere but here. I was charmed to find that Nili could still be so entirely in the now, so much so that she once again thought her dad was being a little strange. The moment was also poignant, though, because I knew that with each passing day, she would find being so absorbed in the present a little more difficult. Her mind would be more and more overtaken by mindwandering, plunging her into ruminations about the past and yanking her into speculations about the future, circling around worries about what her friends are thinking of her and musing about that boy in class who's so cute.

Still Motion in Mind

I am not a religious person, but I do not work on Yom Kippur. As the last one was just about to embark upon us, I was trying to finish writing some paragraph but instead found myself staring out of the window at the bright silver moon. I then told myself I would finish the paragraph quickly and spend the remainder of the thirty minutes left before the holiday began gazing at and enjoying that beautiful moon. So I finished, closed my laptop, opened the window wide, adjusted my chair, and sat to dedicate the next minutes to cherishing the moon. I quickly realized what I knew all along but refused to admit: I could not stay with the moon. My thoughts quickly wandered.

Let's hold on to that moon example as we examine the potential trajectories our thinking can take. There are several possible scenarios. In the first, we look at the moon, or whatever our target might be, for a second or two, and then without even noticing we resume thinking about what was occupying our mind most recently, as stored in our working memory—be it that paragraph, the plans for the holiday, or just reminiscing about my childhood memories of fasting. In the second scenario, the trajectory drifts from the moon in front of us to other thoughts seamlessly, via a path of associations. Look at that gorgeous moon ➙ that *First Man* movie about Neil Armstrong we watched the other night was not bad at all ➙ how could people believe conspiracy theories claiming it did not really happen ➙ like that other theory about Paul McCartney being dead since 1966 ➙ how many times we've tried spinning *Revolution 9* backward in search of that hidden message ➙ and how hard it was to get new music in Israel growing up. You start with the moon, but your mind rides an association wave like it has its own mind. Third, you could be really determined to stay on the moon, so to speak, and, like we do with the breath in meditation, every time you notice you have drifted bring your mind back to the moon. To persist with the moon like that, you will start scrutinizing its elements: the craters, the illusory face, its borders, how much of it is missing to make a full circle, and back again. Just like the body-scan method mentioned earlier, only scanning the moon instead. So you manage to stay focused on the moon, but that's not good enough because we have basically diverted the problem of our mind traveling to other topics to our mind traveling between the features of the moon. In fact, even meditation does not teach us to stay really still because even if we remain with our breath, we do so by monitoring its effect while it flows through our nostrils, how it feels in our body, in and out, surveying continuously. This is still mental movement. The fourth thinking pattern is the holy grail of cherishing the moment, though it is not clear at all that the brain is able to achieve this to the fullest. Just think "moon," without going anywhere. Stay on the concept of "moon" without going back to what has bothered you before your eyes landed on the moon, without thinking about what is associated with the moon in your memory, and without shifting your attention to its elements and properties. Be with its moon-ness. Why can't our mind just say "moon" to itself and then stay still with it, even for just a minute?

It seems virtually impossible, and not only for objects. We cannot stay with a thought after it takes place, and similarly we cannot stay with sentiments and evaluations ("He seems nice," and our mind moves on). There is an excellent reason this is so hard.

Our mind is associative, where one thing leads to another. As elaborated earlier, our entire knowledge, experiences, and everything in memory is connected in a gigantic web. In this web, or semantic network, each concept, fact, or representation is linked with all the others, with different distances (you get from cat to dog in one step; from a cat to a refrigerator in two steps, via milk perhaps; and from a cat to an airplane in more steps). This architecture of massive connectivity confers huge advantages. It allows for easier encoding of memories where they belong the most, connected to other items that are relevant to it, and it also allows for easier retrieval of information from memory because things are connected by topic and by the likelihood of co-occurrence. "Co-occurrence" is jargon worth dwelling on again. Things tend to appear (or occur) in our environment together, in typical arrangements; ovens appear together with refrigerators in kitchens, beach umbrellas and beach chairs tend to appear together on the beach, and so on. This co-occurrence provides the brain with some informative statistics, such that a giraffe is highly likely in a safari but not as likely on the beach. So when we need to retrieve a certain entry from our memory, the search is much easier if items are ordered like that. This memory arrangement is also the foundation for the biggest advantages of them all: our ability to predict. That we are proactive and (almost) always try to anticipate what is next is made possible thanks to associations and associative activation. If you know you are about to enter a kitchen, you'll know what objects to expect and roughly in what spatial arrangement. Similarly, when you go to a job interview, you know how to dress and how to prepare, because knowledge such as this has been stored in your mind associatively when you experienced it in the past. The statistics of what tends to happen in our environment help us remember and help us anticipate.

This proclivity to activate one association after the other is an asset in our lives, but it is also the reason we cannot just look at the moon and be with it and nothing else. Associative movement is compulsory.

The Quality of Our Experience

We walk this earth like aliens. Most of us, most of the time, do feel like we belong, but at the same time we feel detached, each inside our personal skin, trying to fit, but always confined to our own world. We join groups, congregations, and clubs; we cheer for teams and parties; we play by the rules and act according to conventions and do whatever society and culture dictate—all to feel connected, apart yet a part. This results, implicitly or explicitly, in an "I versus the World" attitude, which breeds isolation and makes life a constant struggle. But we now understand that while you are in the world, the world is in you, in your mind. How the world is depends on how your mind is. Your mind determines whether your experience is rich or flat. As individuals, the reflection of the world in our very own mind is the only world there is. We are not outsiders and we are not insiders; we are experiencers.

The idea that what goes on inside our head affects our experience is at the same time trivial and stunning. The pattern of our thoughts, the volume of our mental activity, and our state of mind directly influence how we interpret and feel the world around us, mentally and physically. It seems so intuitive that physical sensations should be absolute and objective that we walk around feeling like they are inflicted on us and that we are merely perceivers, with no say in our experience. Even if we realize that our perceptions are subjective and not "the thing-in-itself," as Kant called it, it is typically easily forgotten, and we are back to playing passive in our own lives. After all, sensors (visual from the eye, somatic from our skin, auditory from our ears, taste from our tongue, or olfactory from our nose) should always respond in the same manner to the same physical stimulation. We expect the same response to the same experience: stimulus → response, like an engineer knowing that the same input to an electrical circuit will always result in the same output, no matter what. But our perception of that stimulus, our subjective experience of it, differs greatly depending on the state of our inner world. We are not just subjects in our moment-to-moment experience. How we feel—how we get goose bumps, scared, blush, enjoy a painting, notice the beauty of dew on a fresh leaf in the morning, appreciate the gradually evolving taste of an orange in our mouth, or our condition as a whole—depends on our state. Experience happens in your brain.

Let's break down an experience to its elements. Take a simple experience, say of watching the shimmering moonlight reflected back to you from a lake. This image enters your eyes and activates cells in your retina, from which it continues through some relay stations and enters your primary visual cortex (the first part of the cortex to receive visual information; there is similarly a primary cortex for each of our other senses). So far this is less an experience and more a mindless response. Consider that a similar response would appear in your primary visual cortex even if you were completely anesthetized and I opened your eyelids for this visual scene to enter your eyes. So, no experience yet.

From there, information, visual in our example, continues to propagate in the visual cortex, with mixed bottom-up, top-down, and even lateral (sideways) influences between neurons. What stage of the cortical response starts to be considered part of the subjective experience? Some middle regions along the visual cortex, the highest regions of the cortical hierarchy in the prefrontal cortex, or perhaps some orchestrated coordination between regions? In philosophy and science of consciousness, the subjective quality of an experience is sometimes called *qualia*. It is that extra stuff you feel when drinking a cold beer on a hot day, or getting a hug from your little daughter, beyond the response to the mere physical features of the event. In addition to the receptors responding to the sound and smell of your daughter, the mechanical pressure of the hug, the tickling of her hair on you face, there is that je ne sais quoi of the experience, the pleasure, that deep warm feeling far removed from the sensory responses proper. It is that quality of the experience that distinguishes how we experience from how a robot or a zombie would.

An experience is a continuum: on the one end there is the lowest level, like the retina and the primary visual cortex that we do not call subjective experience yet, and on the other end there are those elusive qualia at the very top level of subjectivity. We will not worry about the exact line of where the cortical response turns into an experience, if it is even a line at all. It is just to emphasize that an experience has objective as well as subjective aspects. Similarly, it has cognitive as well as emotional aspects, and it has conscious as well as subconscious aspects.

The experience goes beyond understanding what is it that we are perceiving. That shimmering lake also activates memories, associations, feelings, anticipations, and more. All of these are also part of our experience. Those different aspects activate the same as well different brain regions and supply the various facets of the experience. You get a kiss, a slap in the face, a raise, an insult, or an unexpected offer; these human experiences combine cognitive, emotional, and many other aspects that make the experience rich.

One immediate conclusion from this discussion is that an experience needs cortical "real estate" to unfold properly. But such real estate is not always available, given our mind's proclivity to be busy and noisy. Any experience, like the hug from your daughter or the shimmering light reflected from that lake, has infinite details. The more resources we have available in our receiving brain to reflect those details in our mind, as well as to chain-react the memories and emotions associated with those details, the richer is our experience. If most of your mind is taken by your planning of your presentation tomorrow, or by ruminating on an annoying email you just read but are waiting to reply, there is not much left for you to enjoy that hug or that falafel you are eating. Experience and the related thoughts need room to develop.

If your thoughts are elsewhere, there is less for you to experience with. The distracted and the occupied mind takes away from the experience because it uses the exact same work space that we need in order to experience. It is an overlapping space. Move the past and the future from this space, because we need it for the present. Memories, past feelings, future worries—all take the place of present experience and present thoughts.

If you are biting an apple while thinking about the room you need to clean up, some apple-related thoughts and activity will not take place because those neurons are taken by your room-related thoughts. And in that James Bond episode I mentioned earlier: It is not that I did not absorb the chase and the physical stimulation that it emitted into my retinas and eardrums because my mind was somewhere else. I did absorb them in my sensory cortex for sure. But my internally generated mindwandering was so consuming that it took over the cortex I needed for the experience proper. Think of it as no vacancy, no experience; some vacancy, some experience; full vacancy, rich experience. Divided attention simply means divided resources in a zero-sum game.

When studying the possibility of multitasking, we notice that people have a much harder time when the simultaneous tasks are from the same domain. For example, reading text while listening to another text read aloud to us is extremely hard because both tasks require highly overlapping language regions in the brain. Reading while tapping your fingers is much easier because these two tasks require different parts of the cortex. Nevertheless, all parallel processing diminishes the quality of either individual process. This is how we should think of the way in which existing thoughts diminish from the quality of the present experience: a competition between now and elsewhere.

Ongoing State of Mind Flavors Upcoming Experiences

Not only do new experiences need room to unfold with their rich detail, but when they do find their cortical space, they meet there a certain state of mind that is already dominating the overall cortical activity, to which they will have to adhere. New experiences, with whatever richness they were allowed to express themselves, are flavored, not to say tainted, by the ongoing global state of mind. That shimmering lake would be experienced differently depending on not only whether you are available or not, spacewise, but also whether, for example, you are sad or happy at the time it enters your cortex.

This is both bad and good news. It is bad because it adds more distorting factors to our experience, making it even more subjective. Not only do we not see the things as they are because of selective attention, top-down expectations, leaning on memory, prejudice, and so on, and not only that the details are constrained by the limited availability of cortical real estate, but the experience is then flexed and stretched and distorted to cohere with the preexisting state of mind. What chance do we have of seeing the world like the fellow human who stands next to us and absorbs the exact same life event? Slim. Nevertheless, this is also good news because now we know.

Whatever burdens us, consumes us, calls for our attention, guzzles our mental resources, is taking us away from the moments unfolding in front of us. Chief among those parallel processes that rob us of the present is mindwandering, that constant flow of ongoing thoughts, plans, simulations, and ruminations that occupy our mind regardless of our desire. Mindfulness meditation is geared exactly toward minimizing ongoing activity to make more room for new experiences to open their wings in our cortex, while neutralizing state of mind so that those will be the purest experiences.

As William Blake said in *The Marriage of Heaven and Hell*, "If the doors of perception were cleansed every thing would appear to man as it is, Infinite. For man has closed himself up, till he sees all things thro' narrow chinks of his cavern."[1] Indeed, if those doors of perception (after which Aldous Huxley's beautiful book was named and then the band the Doors got its name) are not cleansed of bias and dispositions, it would imply sticking to routines and stereotypical thinking, being exploitatory instead of exploratory, leaning on the past instead of the present, working top-down instead of bottom-up, drawing from memory instead of from our fresh sensations, being there instead of being here.

When my older kids were younger and I would make them breakfast and sit with them to eat, they used to make fun of how deeply zoned out I was, clearly far away with my thoughts. Initially, they were even scared of my expression, an intense yet detached look in my eyes. This is another amazing aspect of mindwandering: not only that we are elsewhere, but that we are strongly committed with our entire mind to that elsewhere. I was a zombie dad, a physical body in the same room and at the same table as they were, but not really there. In that state, how did I experience the conversation, their laughter, the taste of the waffle with maple syrup in my mouth? I was an automaton going through the motions. I am often stunned by how involved I can seem to be in a conversation I am not really attending, responding with sensible answers. And it is not only me. So much of life passes in front of us without our real participation.

Immersion Is Participation

I recently went with Naor to the South of Italy for a few days, to enjoy the beautiful Amalfi Coast with a sweet convertible Fiat Spider. Driving was the highlight, largely because of the manual stick shift, as it turned out. If you've been to the Amalfi Coast, you know that the roads are not only insanely winding but also snug up against the edge of extremely steep rock cliffs. Italian drivers aren't about to slow down for some poky fiftysomething foreigner taking his teenager for a pleasure cruise. I had to devote every little spark of my mental energy, for every millisecond, to not spin out of control and into the Tyrrhenian Sea. Switching gears—one, two, three, four, five, six—I was involved. I was doing the driving. I was the driving. It was absolutely thrilling. It was the most exhilarating, all-encompassing fun I'd had in quite some time. But life, for most of us, for most of the time, is akin to driving on automatic. At a certain age we know enough to turn to automatic, to gradually switch our life to D. It mostly drives by itself, and we are the passive passengers.

Why, exactly, does being so immersed make us feel so alive? The answer, in short, is that immersion is a bottom-up-only state, all sensing and responding, no mental comments. When we are immersed in an experience, we do not think about the experience. We do not think, period. The world transmits and your mind responds: no mindwandering, no expectations, no divided resources, no judgments, and no deliberations. Rather than being narrowly focused on a certain aspect of your environment, external or internal, you are broadly open to anything, and feeling everything.

Immersion is a key ingredient for enjoyable life and satisfying experiences, but it is not what mindfulness meditation teaches us to be. What mindfulness meditation teaches us is to be aware of the present, observe and witness, be here and now. This is essential, but not sufficient. It is up to us to participate in our lives. We are not bystanders in our experience, and we are not coaches or scientists with a clipboard observing, commenting, and interpreting. We want to jump in and feel firsthand. When we truly immerse ourselves in an activity, we're too engaged to observe ourselves. One comes at the expense of the other; if we observe more we are less immersed, and if we are more immersed we observe less.

The mindfulness dilemma mentioned earlier is that being mindful makes us witnesses and observers, but not necessarily immersed. Our mind is in the present both when we're mindful and when we're immersed, but when we're immersed, we are not aware of that. In immersion, for good or for bad, we are lost in our experience.

By saying we are lost, I'm not just being metaphoric. We lose our sense of self, which can be a wonderfully healthy mind cleanse, forcing your DMN to stop thinking about yourself for a little and to stop with all that inner speech. This is part of the addictive appeal of video games. Game designers aim to immerse players in the game, and players report that when they've been intensely engaged in a game, they felt like they became part of the game. You can even find online lists of games ranked by level of immersion, with *Battlefield V* currently at the number-one spot.

Another thing we lose when we are immersed is the sense of time. In fact, change in time perception has been suggested as one reliable measure of degree of immersion.[2] This effect is seen in reports of Major League Baseball batters who say they perceive a pitch in slow motion. How else could they connect with a fastball averaging ninety miles per hour? We don't know precisely why this loss of sense of time effect happens; the neuroscientific study of immersion is still in its infancy. What is relatively more explored is the related concept of *absorption*.

While immersion is a state, absorption is a trait.[3] In other words, immersion is a temporary, fleeting state, while absorption is a personality

trait of a general tendency for immersion, although they are understandably often used interchangeably. A person with a high score on the trait
of absorption will be immersed more often. Of the traditional Big Five
personality measures, it has been found that openness to experience and
extraversion are positively correlated with the tendency for immersion.[4]
Interestingly, absorption is also positively correlated with hallucinations
and delusions, so participants with psychosis are significantly higher on
absorption.[5] The trait of absorption is also a reliable predictor of spiritual
and religious experiences. Overall, both immersion and absorption are
linked with embracing an experience.

During immersion and absorption, the DMN is considerably less active.[6] It makes sense that if we lose ourselves when immersed, there will
be less activity in the network involved with thinking about the self. It
seems that when your mind is so dedicated to the experience in front
of you, barely a shred of neuronal activity is allocated to anything else,
particularly to mindwandering. Of course, following the discussion in
the previous chapters, another critical condition for an immersive experience is the shutting off of top-down influences. Expectations, desires,
plans, projections from memory, and labeling things with names all
stand in the way of immersion. Reduced top-down and reduced mindwandering and DMN activity are central for immersion.

As we saw before, mindfulness meditation also reduces DMN activity and wandering about the self. The difference is that in meditation,
they are reduced to free up mental space for future experiences. In immersion, on the other hand, the reduction of DMN activity and mindwandering serves for direct participation in the present experience. In
immersion the default activity subsides so that those mental resources
can be diverted toward the stimulating, immersive, all-encompassing
experience. Immersion is exhilarating. In meditation, self and other
thoughts evaporate (through labeling, for example) for a more general

emptiness. One distinction is highlighted by the fact that if we have a thought about our self while we're meditating, we just let it come and go, but if we're made aware of our self somehow while we're having an immersive experience, we will be pulled out of it. Here's a silly example. For whatever reason, I tend to find myself in places where I am the oldest person. Dance clubs, CrossFit training, yoga, or fun Tel Aviv restaurants: I throw myself into these opportunities to become immersed, in music, physical exertion, or conversation. I don't think about the age difference or that I look awkward. But if someone makes any sort of comment that raises the specter of age, that's it; I become highly aware of the fact that I am the only one with gray hair, that I'm so much less flexible, or that I have more degrees than almost everyone around me. The problem is, though, that becoming self-aware is usually just a tiny step away from becoming self-conscious. I start to feel like I'm being stared at by everyone. Then I realize that, in effect, I'm staring at myself. Immersion turns into observation, and there goes all the joy.

The loss of a sense of self and of time has also been reported as a part of the experience of *flow*, which may seem highly related to immersion. There's been surprisingly little solid neuroscience research on flow since Mihaly Csikszentmihalyi introduced the concept in the seventies.[7] Csikszentmihalyi describes it as a state of deep engagement in a task that our brains get into when there is a proper balance between the skill we bring to it and the degree of challenge. It's considered so advantageous for performance in sports that athletes are sometimes given neurofeedback training in flow. One big difference is that immersion is not confined to positive experiences. You will be immersed in the experience of pushing your car breaks frantically to avoid a collision. Flow also involves performing a certain task, and we've got to feel challenged, whereas with immersion, we can just be swept away in a moment-to-moment experience, such as a zip-line ride, or a kiss, without the pursuit of a specific goal.

At the risk of overwhelming with concepts and psychological phenomena, I will describe an interesting link between immersion and *semantic satiation*. In semantic satiation, the repetition of a certain word makes it temporarily lose its meaning. Try saying "avocado" fifty times, and you will notice that you gradually hear only "meaningless" sounds. According to the framework presented here, top-down influences subside with repetitions, and with them references to memories of things we already know, and we are left only with the sounds arriving at us bottom-up from the senses. This is also reminiscent of the artistic practice of estrangement, defamiliarization, or *ostranenie* in Russian (coined by the Russian formalist Viktor Shklovsky in his essay from 1917 "Art as Technique"), where familiar characters, objects, or concepts are presented in a strange way, detached from their original meaning, to create a new perspective with which to view them. With no top-down involvement, we are immersed in the physical stimulation. With that total attention to our senses, no wonder that immersion and a "sense of presence" also promote better perceptual sensitivity to minute physical details we are less likely to notice otherwise.[8]

One opposite of the state of immersion is a state of boredom. You will be surprised how much research there is on the topic of boredom. Boredom is often mentioned in the context of ADHD, specifically that individuals with ADHD have a lower tolerance for boring tasks (hell yeah!). ADHD seems to vanish in immersive situations. Kids with attention problems seem to be completely attentive when the experience interests them enough to be immersed.

The potential for immersive experience is a terrible thing to waste. Our brains evolved for the DMN to hog their bandwidth, and for good reasons, but they also evolved to give us this extraordinary pleasure from short-circuiting it.

Think Less, Experience Better

It is a good opportunity now to divulge that one trigger for writing this book is a piece I wrote for the *New York Times* in June 2016, titled "Think Less, Think Better." The interest it garnered made it clear that these ideas struck a chord with quite a few readers. We, obviously, care about the quality of our experience, and we are not happy with the current state of affairs. The main points of that piece were that most of us are bystanders in our own lives; that without immersion, experience is shallow; that an occupied mind, busy with worries, ruminations, or simply loaded with ongoing information, diminishes the quality of experience.

Why "think less"? It's not only because the quality of experience is enhanced with the increased availability of mental resources and cortical "real estate," but also because the capacity for original and creative thinking is clogged by the presence of many thoughts and all types of mental interferences. By default, we are a creative and innovative species. It is just everyday mental junk that takes these awesome capabilities away from us. Recently, I hosted Israel's most creative chef and one of the most interesting people I have ever met, Eyal Shani, on the Bar-Ilan campus for an evening discussion on creativity. The event was sold out instantly, and our auditorium was packed like never before. In my opening remarks, I told the audience about the fascination of people I have observed over the years with the topic of creativity. I do not think the turnout would have been so great and enthusiastic even if the topic of the event were instead "How to Add Fifteen Years to Your Life." And there is a hopeful and happy sentiment in here: our natural tendency is to explore and to learn. We want to create: not to eat more, not to sleep more, and not to watch more TV; we would rather create than do all of these.

By now we realize there are multiple sources for diminishing the quality of our experience, all of which we need to fight for better experiences in our lives. First, the quality of our experience is tainted and possibly tarnished because the doors of our perception are not cleansed: dispositions, biases, prejudice, convictions, and strong expectations all affect how we see the world. Second, the depth and richness of our lives are dramatically reduced by our tendency to occupy our mind and multitask, that false belief that we can do multiple things at once. Indeed, trying to do (which includes also to think) only one thing at a time is an excruciating exercise. And the multiple demands on our mental capacities are not always a matter of voluntary and conscious choice. Third, and perhaps the most profound factor, is the lack of immersion. We can't be always watching and narrating our life; we need to be inside our life.

Let's repeat these key obstacles for experiencing life to the fullest: top-down dispositions, mental load, and not being immersed. The best method I know to abolish these obstacles is mindfulness meditation, but I am sure there are more. Mindfulness unites our responses to the outer and inner world; it diminishes dispositions and other top-down influences that make us prejudiced, judgmental, and demanding of the world; and it helps us focus on the present. The term "emptiness" in Buddhism doesn't mean an empty mind; it means a mind empty of distortions. Regarding immersion, that's another story.

Overall, understanding mindfulness is understanding how thoughts affect quality of experience. Mindfulness in itself does not make us happy; it just makes us be aware of what is going on, good or bad, so that we can experience life as it comes.

Happiness Redux

A few years ago, I was invited to give a talk in Rio de Janeiro, at a scientific meeting on computer vision. On one of the evenings, the hosts took us to see a soccer game in the famous Maracanã stadium, between Flamengo and Vasco de Gama. I am not a soccer fan, but it is Brazil, and the Maracanã—what could I say? The atmosphere in the stadium was electrifying, not to say dangerous. On the way out at the end of the game we saw a shirtless fan dancing and singing with exceptional joy, his obviously drunk facial expression showing he was in a world of sheer happiness, not in ours. Sven, my colleague from Canada, turned to me and said, "Moshe, what would it take for you to be that happy?" Sadly, I could not think of anything. With the exception of Malcolm Butler's last-second interception in Super Bowl XLIX, and perhaps a couple more, I could not think of a single moment I was so ecstatic. Happy, sure, many times, but deep, unobstructed, carefree happiness is something we do not experience much once we grow up.

For her fifteenth birthday, my daughter joined me at another scientific meeting, this time on aesthetics and the brain, in Frankfurt. Part of her birthday present was that we both went to a Harry Styles concert. I and fifteen thousand teenage girls gathered excitedly. The crowd and the behavior around were fascinating. For a neuroscientist interested in human nature, this was a giant petri dish of teenage cosmos and true happiness. I was examining the kids: their expressions, their body language, their conversations, and their restless anticipation for Mr. Styles. I have never been surrounded by so much joy. From the waiting period through the show and until its end, there was such immense happiness and freedom in the air that I truly came to believe megastars such as Harry Styles deserve a place of honor in our society for the health and well-being benefits they bring about. (Apparently, Styles had just come out as liking women and men alike a month or so before, liberating thousands of confused teenagers who were now feeling so proud and free to come to a show covered with the colorful gay flag. Rivers of agony, money, and time with therapists were saved in a single human gesture by their talented idol.)

But I would like to focus on the individual joy. I saw two girls as they arrived at their seats, and I could recognize the moment it dawned on them they were actually about to see Styles. They looked at each other with such deep happiness. An expression quite like this I have not seen in adults for ages. No amount of money or achievement would have brought such intense expression of happiness to my friends' faces, not even a phone call from the Nobel Prize Committee. It stayed with me for the entire show and ever since. Those two naive, beaming, genuinely happy faces.

And in my choice of the word "naive" lies the problem. Why is it that only the childish and naive can be so extremely happy? How is it that we have accepted subhappiness as our fate? Demanding to replicate the extreme happiness of years gone by, on a daily basis, should not be dismissed as unrealistic.

Happiness has proven to be an increasingly elusive target. At Harvard University, and later also at Yale, the courses that have drawn the highest number of students, by a huge margin, are two courses about happiness. We are suckers for anything that promises us happiness. This is obviously a constant quest of the human race. We are an unhappy race, desperate for ways to make things better. So, of course, asking for extreme happiness like I do here may seem greedy, if not delusional. But I do think that we should all ask where extreme happiness has gone with age.

Central as happiness is to our being, there is no scientific definition for the concept. There is hardly a definition for mood. In the present context, what we have seen so far is that how we think affects how we feel, and how we feel affects how we think. Mental activity determines our state of being. It gives me comfort to know that my brain is responsible for my happiness.

CHAPTER TWELVE

AN OPTIMAL MIND
FOR THE OCCASION

YOU SIT IN A MEDITATION ROOM, WITH THIRTY TO FORTY OTHERS, SILENT, on pillows and little rugs. You focus on your breath for forty-five minutes, and it is all immensely relaxing. You are deep in thought—or hopefully observing your thoughts, rather—eyes closed. You hear birds from a distance, and overall you are feeling as if you are on a cloud. It is almost noon, although you have absolutely no sense of time, and you have been doing this on and off since six in the morning. Suddenly, you hear the Tibetan Bowl gong. It is not loud, but it is assertive. The session is over. In an instant, your body and mind change completely. Your brain immediately fills with what is ahead: taking your shoes and bottle of water from outside the room and rushing to the dining hall before the food is gone. (Well, you can tell I am not enlightened yet . . .)

You feel your muscles tense, and your mind is certainly not on a cloud anymore. In just a second, your being has been totally transformed, from inward to outward, from now to next, from passive to active, all at once, and all engulfing.

One late night during a family trip to Moscow (insight strikes when you are least expecting), I reflected on all of the findings previously discussed—about mindwandering, prediction, perception, mindfulness, the appeal of the novel, broadly associative thinking, mood, and immersion—and suddenly realized that all these different dimensions are connected and together make up our state of mind. They are bundled together and changing in tandem along a spectrum between two opposing states of mind.

Overarching States of Mind

We are dynamic and versatile organisms, adapted to fit multiple scenarios and numerous situations. Unlike what intuition might have us believe, our mind is not fixed. Just like our pupil can dilate to match optimally a specific level of light, our entire mind can change depending on task and context.

"State of mind" is not just a figure of speech: it is all encompassing, and it is dynamic. Consider the following dimensions along which our state of mind can be varying: we can be highly creative and think in broad associations or think narrowly and be intensely focused; we can attend, perceive, and remember the global properties (the "forest") or the local properties ("trees") of the world around us; our perception can be influenced by bottom-up incoming information or by top-down predictions and biases; our mood can be positive (up to manic) or negative (down to depressed); we can be in the now (like in mindfulness meditation) or mentally travel in time to the past or to the future; we can be thinking inwardly about self-related topics or oriented in our mind more outwardly to our surroundings; and when it comes to our motivation to learn, experience, and tolerate uncertainty, we can be exploratory of the novel or exploitatory of the familiar. These are all continuous spectrums, moving from Broad to Narrow (or from Open to Closed). Our mind is rarely at either extreme, but they need to be understood and taken into account when trying to explain the human mind.

The central message in this new framework of states of mind, developed with Noa Herz, is twofold: our state is dynamic, and it is overarching in that all those facets—perception, attention, thinking, openness, and affect—move in orchestration with a change of state.[1] These different states of mind entail different sets of biases and dispositions, which can exert substantial and ubiquitous effects on our perception, cognition, thought, mood, and action. States of mind can literally change our subjective experience of the environment and of our very being. It is as fascinating as it is important to realize that the brain can have "states," aligning different mental processes in accordance with the demands of the current situation, like a web cast over our entire mind.

If one is in the midst of a creative burst of thought, for example, she is also broadly associative in her thinking; her mindwandering will be wide ranging; she'll be in a positive mood, attending to and perceiving the world around her in a more global, bottom-up, and exploratory manner; and she'll have heightened sensitivity to the novel. This is what I have dubbed the Broad and Open state of mind. By contrast, if she is focusing in a top-down way on making use of memory to get a task done, she is also considering a more limited range of information, preferring routine, thinking more stereotypically, and avoiding novelty and uncertainty. If her mind is wandering, it will be doing so narrowly. This is the Narrow and Closed state of mind.

One less intuitive aspect that the concept of a state of mind entails is that it contains information about the future. Usually, when you measure a phenomenon of nature, with whatever sophisticated measuring tools you might have, you can gauge the studied system about its current state: how it is doing right now, like what the current temperature in the room is, the magnitude of the light coming out of a bulb, or the exact amount of sugar in the coffee you are drinking. And that's informative. Sometimes measurements also contain information about the past state of that system, like how an EKG can tell a cardiologist information about past dynamics of the heart, or like how we know that the light we see coming from a star far away from us has been emitted so many light-years ago, and sometimes that star no longer even exists by the time its light reaches us. In fact, simply by enjoying a sunset your eyes perform a measurement, of light and color, of a sunset that happened a few minutes earlier. State of mind, however, also contains information about you in the future: how you are likely to respond, to feel, or to act in the face of different triggers and stimulations based on your current state. It is as if you could predict the upcoming performance of the stock market based on how it is doing now. If we had perfect mind-measuring tools, your state right now (Open and Broad, for example) would help anticipate your originality in solving an upcoming problem or whether you are more or less likely to take risks. Your current state predicts your future self.

States of mind are different from personality traits, which obviously also affect dispositions, attitudes, behavior, and performance. An impatient person will be less likely to be focused for long durations, and a person rated high on the Big Five's personality measure of "openness to experience" is more likely to exhibit exploratory behavior than exploitatory, safe actions. One can think of personality as the envelope and SoM as the individual's fluctuations within this envelope. States of mind are more transitory, and as such less continuous, but they are equally influential. Take mood, for example. Whether you are happy or sad at the moment would directly affect faculties such as your current scope of attention, memory, and more. Similarly, whether your working memory is loaded, like when you have to memorize a long string of digits before you find a pen and paper, or when you simply have a lot on your mind, would directly affect how creative you are during that time and how exploratory or exploitatory you would be. This in turn would affect also how readily you will detect novelty in your environment and how much risk you will be taking when making decisions during that state.

William Hutchison Murray, inspired by John Anster's loose translation of Goethe's *Faust*, wrote, "Whatever you can do, or dream you can do, begin it. Boldness has genius, power, and magic in it. Begin it now."[2] I love this quote. Those powerful words can move one into action, instill determination, change a state of mind radically: words, taking you from state A to state B. Indeed, states of mind can change by various triggers, making us pretty adaptive and dynamic creatures.

Say you are a team manager and you have decided to hold a brainstorming session with your group. You've got a big problem you need a really creative solution for; it's been haunting you for weeks and a collective hashing out just might do the trick. The question is, how can you get people to truly put their creativity into it?

Well, would you be considering what sort of state of mind your team members should be in as they head into the session? You certainly should. Would you be thinking that you want them to be buckled down, ready to really focus? No chitchat, no donuts or pizza: you want them in serious problem-solving mode. Think again. We've just discussed how people in a good mood tend to be more creative, better at solving problems requiring novel insights, because when we're happy, our minds go into the broadly associative mode. So you would want them to be upbeat, to be feeling like the session will be fun. You could set the tone by showing a clip from a Monty Python movie or maybe a hilarious cat video. How unexpected. Get them laughing, and then toss the problem out to them. This is just one small example of a process that we can all incorporate in our daily lives—orchestrating our state of mind, working to tune it to the demands of the moment.

Let us consider immersion again, this time in the context of the overarching states-of-mind framework. Immersion is the extreme of the exploratory state, all bottom-up receiving with no top-down imposition of memories, familiar associations, or expectations. At the other extreme, full exploitation, if this is ever possible, not a single neuron would be responding to external stimulation from the environment. All processing would be of information and sensations from within. I'd like to see if such a state can be induced so that we can study it, and so my lab is purchasing sensory deprivation tanks, in which people float in the dark in water at skin temperature and there is no external sound, light, or any other physical stimulation.

Once I had that insight about the interconnections of our mental experience in each state, it seemed as though this should have been obvious all along. Yet it had to emerge this way because of how compartmentalized research on the brain is. As a student you learn that perception is one field of research, attention is another, as are memory and mood. As a researcher, you tend to specialize in one of the fields, and that makes it difficult to see how they connect. But because I'd been drawn by various findings in areas outside my initial expertise to move across those divides in my lab, the dots ultimately came together. Seeing, at last, how they all fit into a clear picture was my most exciting discovery so far. That was true not only because of the sheer scientific joy of solving a bedeviling puzzle, but because it was immediately apparent to me that this realization could be helpful in our daily lives. Understanding this spectrum can guide us in working to move our minds purposefully one way or the other along it.

Exploration Versus Exploitation

When I used to take the kids to the Museum of Science in Boston and we were going to the cafeteria for lunch, I liked to sit them close to the entrance and show them something peculiar about the human mind. People who walked in stared at our plates, while people who walked out looked at our faces. It was a striking difference between states: hunger for food information and hunger for social information. Outside of survival, human beings strive to maximize reward. The more reward, the merrier. What we find rewarding depends on our state: sometimes food, sometimes sex, sometimes learning, and sometimes a pleasant routine. Curiously, even basic perception depends on those states of mind. We tend to have the subjective impression that we perceive our environment, entirely, continuously, and homogenously, always in the same manner. But the truth is that our perception is guided, constrained, and distorted by more influences than could be appreciated.

Our needs, goals, and intentions are powerful drives that dictate what we collect with our senses from the scene around us. If you are rushing to catch a departing bus you are less likely to notice the aesthetics of a building on your way, if you are focused on someone's beautiful face you may later have trouble recalling the color of that person's shirt, and when you are enjoying the view of a forest you will have a hard time noticing changes to individual trees. Indeed, the scope with which we examine our environment has been shown to vary as a function of factors such as task, context, and even mood.

If our state of mind affects our behavior and our very perceptions so directly, one would like to know what determines those powerful states of mind. Beyond goals and intentions, one force that establishes our state is the interesting tension in the brain between "exploration" and "exploitation." In many respects, these two extremes differ in how tolerant we are to uncertainty in each.

In everyday life there is a healthy balance between these two extremes. We need them both; if we were not somewhat exploratory, we could not learn and develop, and if we were not exploiting the certainty of the familiar when necessary, we would have a hard time surviving. The neural underpinnings that subserve exploration and exploitation, as well as the neurotransmitters and related mechanisms that make us switch between them, are being actively studied and gradually revealed. Our evolving knowledge will ultimately have important implications for our everyday lives. Beyond understanding the cortical underpinnings, it is important for all of us to recognize where we are on the exploration-exploitation spectrum and occasionally steer our activities accordingly. If you need to balance a detailed budget sheet, it is better to do it while you are in a more exploitatory mode. But looking for a creative name for your new company might benefit best from an exploratory mode.

These states, and the tension between them, not only guide our interaction with the outside world, but pertain to our inner mental lives as well. In line with the scientific research that shows parallels between the inside and the outside of our mental lives, as well as with Buddhist teachings that there is no real distinction between inside and outside, the border seems arbitrary. As Shunryu Suzuki says in his excellent book *Zen Mind, Beginner's Mind*, it is more like a revolving door than a wall between our internal and external worlds. From a more scientific perspective, they are not separate because the outside world is perceived, represented, and exists in our own internal world. Just like our disposition toward the external world around us, our internal thinking pattern can also change between open and wide in the exploratory state to closed and narrow in the exploitatory state. We can be focused on a certain thought or problem, or we can roam associatively from one topic to another. A lot of what our brain is doing when we are not busy with a demanding task, when we wander, is planning and generating "what-if" simulations. These usually result in scripts that can help us cope with upcoming situations. The more exploratory our thinking pattern is, the broader and more intense those simulations are expected to be. An exploratory mind is a creative mind, but it is not the only mind we need. We need to close our mind to distractions when we are focused, but we also need to be open to new occurrences we have not anticipated. Focused yet open-minded is a delicate balance. Louis Pasteur said that chance favors the prepared mind. The mind that is most prepared to notice chance encounters is the exploratory mind, but the mind that is then required to pursue this encounter productively is an exploitatory mind.

More research is required before we know how best to utilize this important tension to optimize performance and well-being. But beyond improving daily activities, there are implications for prevalent mental disorders, and I will mention two.

As described before, the hallmark of most types of mood disorders such as depression and anxiety is a ruminative thinking pattern. Ruminations are cyclical, constricted to a narrow topic, and are difficult to stop. To be creative and productive, the mind needs to be broadly associative, but the depressed and anxious mind is often the opposite. As such, individuals with major depression and anxiety disorder spend most of their mental activities in an exploitation mode. Rumination is like a task that demands resources, and it thus loads and robs our mind.

On the other end of this spectrum there are individuals with ADHD, the ultimate explorers of their environment, noticing almost everything, while committing to almost none. Such individuals could have benefited from a somewhat improved ability to dwell, while individuals with a ruminative mind could have benefited from a more broadly associative mind. This is a topic of current research in my laboratory, modulating the balance between exploration and exploitation for the sake of improved mood and for a more precise understanding of this central tension inside our brains. Nevertheless, it could already be proposed that lives will be lived better by understanding the respective strengths and dispositions of such diverse minds.

The Stuff of States of Mind

It is not completely possible to explain how states of mind are made yet, but it is important to keep in mind that there are different levels of explanation. One can look at molecules, especially those messenger neurotransmitters, on the lowest end, or one can look instead at behavior and mental events on the other, highest, end of the explanation level hierarchy. In between one can consider intermediate neuroscientific accounts of neurons, circuits, and physiological activations.

What determines our state of mind? There are many factors, including context, goals, and history. State of mind could be determined by an external trigger, such as witnessing a tragic road accident or receiving wonderful news, or it could be determined by internal events, such as arising thoughts or bodily sensations. There is one overarching hypothesis with which most, if not all, states of mind could be explained: our state of mind is determined by the balance between top-down processing and bottom-up processing in the brain.

The cortical meaning of top-down and bottom-up processing was explained in more detail earlier but noted in intuitive terms again here. Top-down processing means reliance on past experience, memory, context, goals, and predictions, which precede and shape perception by streaming down from high cortical levels that store all this accumulated knowledge. Bottom-up processing, on the other hand, conveys the direct input from our senses, without facilitation (and possible distortion) from higher areas in the cortical hierarchy, simply the cortical responses to the physical stimulation perceived from the environment. In most perceptions, cognitions, emotions, and actions, our brains operate by combining both top-down and bottom-up influences to different degrees, with different relative emphases assigned to the downstream and upstream effects depending on a host of factors.

It is informative to consider the extremes, however. When is processing in the brain completely top-down, with no weight given to the bottom-up signals at all? Dreaming is one example, where there is no sensory input to generate bottom-up influences (of course, there are always exceptions). Daydreaming is also close to being mostly but not completely top-down. Another such illustration involves mental imagery. If you are asked to close your eyes and imagine the arrangement of the furniture in your apartment, or imagine your friend with blue hair and bright yellow clothes, you do it solely based on top-down processing with no bottom-up information. (Interestingly, people with *aphantasia*, the inability to experience mental images, which often take the rest of us adrift, report being more in the present and experience fewer episodes of mindwandering.)[3]

The best example for the other extreme, of bottom-up only with no weight given for top-down signals, is true mindfulness. Theoretically, in "successful" meditation, with enough practice, and the desired highest standard of full mindfulness, top-down processes are turned off. This is indeed how I see meditation works, helping us appreciate the very present by diminishing the involvement of top-down processes that take us elsewhere in time and space, being able to enjoy looking at that bird on a tree in front of us, uninterrupted and unbothered by concerns, goals, judgments, and expectations.

How much top-down information is taken into account and how much bottom-up determines your state of mind at that moment. Whether you consume your environment with a broad and open spotlight of attention or through a focused peephole, whether you will take risks or stick to the familiar, whether you will be thinking creatively with broad associations or ruminate on the same topic, whether you will be happy or sad: all depend on the current balance between top-down and bottom-up processes in your brain, whether you assign more weight to what is coming in through the senses or to what flows downward within. Where you are on the spectrum of this balance determines how you perceive, process, and feel on all those dimensions at once. But we should not let the language used here confuse us into thinking that we are in perfect control of our state of mind. Most of it is automatic and outside the realm of consciousness or voluntary control, triggered by external cues from our environment and by internal signals and thoughts. But nevertheless, we do have some influence on our state of mind, and by understanding it we can increase our say in our state.

Changing States

States of mind are not destiny. They can change, deliberately or not. In many respects, changing a state of mind is akin to the psychological concept of reframing. We can look at the same situation in different ways, and how we choose (or accept) to look at it can affect our entire attitude toward it. As an exercise, imagine how differently you will feel and behave when meeting a new person if she is interviewing you for a job, you are interviewing her for a job, or this is your first date. A state of mind can affect not only our actions but also our perceptions. Even a basic perception such as the passage of time can subjectively be perceived as slow if you are bored or suffering or perceived as passing quickly if you are exhilarated, although we know it is always the same.

States of mind can sometimes be changed voluntarily, like we do in the laboratory with SoM inductions. We can change mood, breadth of thought, the scope of attention, global versus local perception, exploratory or exploitatory attitudes, and so on. Importantly, because all those different dimensions are linked together, changing one changes the others accordingly. If you make one happier, that person will also think more broadly and associatively, perceive the environment more globally, with a wider attentional scope, and will be more tolerant of uncertainty. And if you make one think more broadly associatively, you would also improve her mood, and so on. They are tied together, which could be used to our advantage when changing one property is difficult but could be accessed indirectly through another property that is linked to it. It is like having multiple entry points to the same state. You cannot necessarily tell someone to be creative on demand, but you can improve their mood and thus affect also associative thinking and creativity for the better.

Becoming familiar with ways of gauging your state of mind can help you optimize activities per state. In an example from another domain, I know when I sleep very little I can be easily irritable (and annoying) during the day. When I recognize that state, I tell myself explicitly to minimize interactions with people and to keep my email writing to a minimum, just like you do not want the happy music at the store to influence you into buying more just because you are feeling cheerful and less restrained. States of mind, and their manipulation, can also be harnessed for better performance. When you are in a happy mood, it is hard to sit still, and thus it is not the best state for working on your tax returns (when is it ever?), and it is also good to know that when you are in this state decisions you'll make will tend to be riskier. It is, however, the best state for coming up with a nonconventional solution for a problem. The same way that you know that your best time of the day for concentration is in the morning, know that your best state for exploring new territories without anxiety is the state of broadly associative thinking.

One more interesting aspect about states of mind has to do with memory and the limit of mental simulations. In some states our ability to imagine an alternative state is stunningly limited. A person in a depressive episode feels miserable and often cannot visualize herself feeling better. Just ask her to imagine how good she felt yesterday, and you will see she has no real notion. A depressing state of mind is so engulfing that it takes over the memory of other states. Similarly, it makes it impossible to imagine a future of feeling better. It also works in the other direction: You wake up to a sunny day, and when you suddenly recall you were awake in the middle of the night for a long hour worried about little things, you just cannot understand how such nonsense tormented you so deeply. When you were in it, though, it all seemed so real, substantial, and worrisome. When you are out of it, you can no longer relive the strength of those feelings.

This issue of our inability to relive, or just refeel, can explain something more profound about our everyday experience and well-being. In the Buddhist instructions that encourage us to be in the moment and experience the present, we are usually reminded that being in the past is just not good for us. It is based on memory of past experiences, but memory is not experience. When you reactivate a memory of an experience, it is the memory, not the experience itself with all its actual sensations and the feelings that it evoked when it took place. It is a shallow representation of experience, without most of the colors, tastes, and sounds and without the emotional depths that were experienced when that past was present. What this discussion implies is that at least part of the reason we cannot refeel the way we felt while the remembered experience took place is because of a collision between how we feel now and how we felt then, between our remembered state and our current state. We simply cannot contain them both simultaneously because they compete for the same cortical real estate. In perception, there is a concept of bistable figures and bistable perception, like the famous young and old women illusion, where you can hold only one perception in your mind at a given moment: you see either the old woman or the young woman, and though your perception can alternate between these interpretations, you cannot hold both at once. This is also the case with holding in mind two states. You are either here or there, but you cannot experience both at once. The present state and feelings dominate, and the reactivated ones from memory are limited to a reduced version, less palpable, like a picture on a screen.

There are other instances of our need and (in)ability to hold two opposing views in the same mind. Blaise Pascal said in *Pensées* that man is equally incapable of seeing the nothingness from which he emerges and the infinity in which he is engulfed. My upbringing by two very young parents was a blessing full of contradictions. At times they made me feel like I could do anything and achieve whatever I aimed for in this world, and at other times they made me feel like a loser who should learn what being humble means. It was pretty confusing, but it ended up being a useful tool throughout my life. And it turned out that, unbeknownst to them, this creed had already been preached by the Hasidic Jews. It is said that Rabbi Bunam told his students that each person should carry two notes. One note would say "The world was created for me," and the other note should say "I am only earth and ashes."

Obviously, neither could work alone; we cannot walk this life always thinking the world was created for us, and we cannot always think of ourselves as "ashes." So we live our lives with both ways of looking at ourselves and alternate between the two. Depending on context, on our needs, on our specific dispositions that moment, we can feel more one than the other. But we have both notes with us, like those alternating bistable visual illusions or like alternating between states of mind.

Broad and Open Versus Narrow and Closed States of Mind

It becomes clear that states of mind are a package deal, a set of tendencies and dispositions tied together. Being creative, broadly associative, in a positive mood, attending and perceiving the world globally, more exploratory, more curious, seek thrills, and be less influenced by top-down processes: all go hand in hand. We call this a Broad (or Open) state of mind. On the other hand, in a Narrow (or Closed) state of mind, people are more focused, less associative, attending the local elements of the world more analytically, exploitatory, preferring routine, leaning on memory, and avoiding novelty and uncertainty.

(I once heard the late Francis Crick, a Nobel laureate together with James Watson for codiscovering the structure of DNA, say that reading rots the mind. Most people around the dinner table were puzzled by this statement, but it resonated with me instantly. When I start a new research project in a domain that is new to me, I prefer not to read the existing literature on the subject so that my thinking remains fresh and unaffected. I read later, of course, but I do not want anything people have said before to shape my thinking into old patterns that already dominate the specific field I am entering before my thoughts are formed. It usually works fine. One occasion where I did find after the fact that thoughts similar to mine had been raised before in some form was with regards to open and closed states of mind, which came from an unexpected direction: John Cleese, the leader of Monty Python and the brilliant mind behind many great comical as well as cerebral pieces. I will forever cherish the moments of teary laughter that bonded me with my grandfather while watching *Fawlty Towers*, and I feel honored to have been preceded by my childhood idol, who although is not a scientist has been stunningly on point here as well.)

Such radically different states of mind result in radically different perspectives. Take uncertainty, for example. The same uncertainty can breed anxiety when you are in a Narrow state of mind because you would prefer the familiar in this exploitatory state, and it will breed thrill when you are in a Broad state of mind because then you are exploring. How excited I was to try street food with names I did not recognize in Varanasi, and how reluctant I would be to order a dish in a Tel Aviv or Boston restaurant if I did not recognize most if not all of its ingredients. The experience is totally different depending on your state of mind.

There is no good or bad state of mind. Broad and Narrow states of mind refer to different mental emphases, each of which is better suited for different circumstances. If you want to learn, to be curious, to explore, and to create, Broad is for you. But if you would like to accomplish a goal, perhaps pursue in earnest an idea originated while you were in a Broad state, focus, be safe, and certain, then Narrow is what you need. Luckily, we are rarely, if ever, in one of these extremes.

As we go about our days, our minds are dynamically moving along the spectrum between these extreme states, and where on the spectrum we want them to be depends on the situation. Some good news about this dynamic quality of our state of mind is how fluidly our minds generally move along this continuum, and we have multiple angles for nudging them in the way we want them to go. Indeed, if we consciously uplift our mood—maybe by putting on some music we love—we will also move closer to the exploratory state of mind. In my lab, we found that by simply showing people the figures below ("Navon figures," after psychologist David Navon, who designed them originally) and asking them to focus either on the small local letters (*H* and *T*) or on the global forms of the big letters (*F* and *L*), we could narrow or broaden their state of mind, and their mood would follow suit. Similarly, as described earlier, we can change breadth of thought, and thereby mood, with lists of words that expand broadly or are only narrowly related. (As you can guess, soon there will be an app for doing that.)

```
HHHHH          T
H              T
HHHHH          T
H              T
H              TTTTT
```

We've all had experience with how rapidly our state of mind can change. This was one of the most profound experiences for me in the meditation retreat, because even when I'd been working so hard to put my brain into a deeply mindful mode, it would snap right out again. Rapid switches like that can happen to us at any moment. Maybe you've been having a blast, laughing with a friend, and then suddenly realize you forgot to send a report to your boss that was due earlier that day. Maybe a memory of an awful experience flashed through your mind while you were watching a show you love and you launched into ruminating. Just like a gong, the ping of an email can pull us out of a focused state and send our minds off weaving a tangential web of associations. This fluidity can be vexing. But it's also a great gift.

I will be continuing to explore the implications of this realization of overarching states of mind for years, and I hope more of my colleagues in the field will join me in the pursuit. For now, I share the existing findings so that people can begin to draw on them as they go through their daily challenges, which I myself have found so helpful, like allocating time for broadly associative mindwandering or going for a run, which can be such a great mind state changer. Perhaps less expected is that going to an unfamiliar environment to work on a problem is a good way to trigger more exploratory and creative thinking. I often suggest taking advantage of your state of mind rather than trying to change it. If you're in a down mood, for example, that would be a good time to focus on getting a mundane task done that you've been putting off. When I am in a broad and open SoM, I allow myself to stay upbeat and seek out some exploratory activity to take advantage of that mood, or I let my mind wander in hopes of coming up with some good new ideas. I've also started respecting my spontaneous bursts of mindwandering, not letting myself feel guilty about them. If my wandering is becoming ruminative, though, I am usually able to do something to break the spell. Over time, taking a state-of-mind check becomes second nature. I now also make a conscious observation of my mental state during any experience, when I remember, and make the choice of whether I want to observe myself experiencing it or want to immerse in the experience as much as I can instead.

I wish I could say we know what conditions summon spontaneous immersion, but the psychological and neuroscientific studies on that are just beginning. What I can attest to, though, is that we can voluntarily immerse ourselves "on demand" to a great extent. My favorite consciously immersive experiences are the ones I have with my children. Of course, we can't be busy all day diagnosing our state of mind. But we can learn to remind ourselves to do it much more often, and, as I've found, doing so will go a long way toward enhancing our lives.

A Loaded Mind Cannot Be Creative

Our mind, naturally, has a finite capacity in how much it can do at once. (It is also limited in the amount of information that can be stored in memory, and the speed with which information can be processed, among other dimensions.) While multitasking is largely a myth, multiple sources can simultaneously tax brain processes and our mental availability. If you need to hold in memory, say, a list of words, you will have very little resources to absorb new information during that time; if you walk the aisles of a supermarket with two crying toddlers, you will not be able to explore or even notice new products on the shelves; and if you are in the presence of an offensive perfume at the museum, you will have a hard time really enjoying the art in front of you.

We can't help it: our mind is busy with something at all times, and we have gotten used to working with what we have left. Just like hiking with a backpack, we move forward and the load usually does not stop us, though it does burden and sometimes limit us. It can be light or heavy, and it will affect our progress accordingly, but we advance while carrying that load in the background. Background mental processes, of which we can be conscious or not, take up a significant part of our mental capacity. We typically notice the presence of background processes and load only when they've stopped or disappeared, like the relief we feel when the air conditioner pauses, a relief from something we did not know bothered us.

Background processes are, therefore, more than a nuisance. While they can serve a purpose, such as "behind-the-scenes" attempts to solve a puzzle that has been bothering you but you had to stop trying, these loading and taxing background events can dramatically affect our state of mind, our cognitive performance, our creativity and ability to solve problems, our enjoyment of our surroundings, and even our mood.

A refresher on an experiment mentioned earlier and is relevant again here. When we ask participants in our experiments at the lab to keep in mind either a long or a short string of digits while participating in a free-association task, their responses are significantly more creative and original when the load is lower (a shorter string, such as "26") compared with when the load is higher (a longer string, such as "4782941"). For example, if you give these participants the word "sole" as the word with which they need to freely associate, those in the high-load condition would typically respond with "shoe," whereas those in the low load would provide "chewing gum" as a response. Outside of the lab setting, this finding implies that we are more creative with a freer mind.

Interestingly, our ability to appreciate beauty is also diminished when our mind is loaded. Appreciating beauty requires attention, and the more attention, the more beauty we can see. (One may argue that similarly one needs attention to feel pain, and thus our distracted mind becomes a blessing when we need to cope with pain. It could be true, though I am not aware of such scientific finding, and my suspicion is that pain, unlike beauty and pleasure, takes priority because of survival factors and as such calls for your attention much more assertively; it is harder to be absentminded with pain than when facing beauty, unfortunately.) The same sculpture can seem more or less pretty based on what we have going on inside already. So much beauty has been wasted on us at moments of busyness.

What types of mental load are present in our everyday lives, beyond the grocery list or rehearsing a telephone number? Some significant ones, more than most of us are aware. One is our mindwandering, which is nearly permanently going on. Our mind not only wanders when we have nothing better to do, but rather strives to use whatever resources are available even when we are engaged in performing a specific task. Everything you do, think, or perceive is divided and only partially attended and appreciated because a good piece of your mind is typically elsewhere. Mindwandering, as discussed, promotes much of our planning and simulation-based decision making, but along the way it sucks out resources from what is happening to and around us.

Similarly, there are ruminations, both in clinical (depression and anxiety) conditions as well as in healthy conditions. Those repetitive and cyclical thoughts are intense and ongoing. But they are not using separate resources that are dedicated for ruminations; they use the very same resources we need for experiencing life. Like mindwandering, ruminations are a tax on our experience.

We saw that in addition to the effect these background intensive processes of mindwandering and rumination have on our present experience, they also take away our ability to be creative. Because all those dimensions are tied together through the overarching SoM, we can take this finding a step further and think of cognitive load as yet another means for manipulating where we are on the SoM continuum. Being mentally loaded reduces creativity and with it implies a closed, narrow state of mind, with narrow (local) perception and attention, narrow thinking, and a less positive mood, and in an overall exploitatory state. With persistent ruminations as a heavy load, it is harder for a depressed individual to be creative. Reducing cognitive load, on the other hand, because it increases creativity, also makes one more exploratory, broadens perceptual and mental scope, and improves mood.

We want to "think less" to reduce background mental noise, but it seems our mind constantly generates new thoughts for us. This is reminiscent of how we always want to be busy with something. In his magnificent and timeless book *In Praise of Idleness*, Bertrand Russell elaborates on the history and benefits of being idle. But most humans work hard to make themselves constantly busy. We cannot sit still; we absolutely have to be busy, mowing our lawns, washing our cars, or making up activities so that we can stay busy and feel productive. In 1930 economist John Maynard Keynes made the forecast in *Economic Possibilities for Our Grandchildren* that by now we would be working only three hours per day to satisfy all our needs. We and technology would be so advanced and efficient that we would have much more free time to do other things we love. But here we are, working harder than ever. Busy we are, inside and out; thoughts fill up our minds like activities fill up our days.

Yesterday evening I took my little Nili to the beach. It was an hour before sunset, during the tail of the season so there were hardly any other people, with a calm sea and a pleasant breeze bringing the fresh smell of the Mediterranean, just me and my girl, skipping and laughing. I seriously cannot imagine anything closer to paradise than that. But then I had to turn it into a photo shoot, asking Nili to pose, taking tens of pictures, and sending them to the family in almost real time. As if this was not enough to take away from that paradise feeling that should not have been meddled with in any event, we started collecting shells from the beach. A couple wouldn't do; I had to go and find a box. And now it became a project, almost work; we were on a mission to fill that box. We forgot about the sea, the sun, and paradise. What was wrong with that initial perfection that we had to fill our relaxed pleasure with activity?

Similarly, our brains could think of nonsense to no end. But by "think less," it is not meant "do not think at all." Creativity is an intricate business. On the one hand, we need to silence the noise so that we have all available resources for the act of creating something new and useful. On the other hand, we need some associative activations and to mentally cover multiple semantic branches in our memory in order to explore and discover. One myth about creativity is that either you have it or you don't, a gift from birth. However, time and again we see evidence that creativity can be learned, trained, and maximized. Of course, one cannot turn into Leonardo da Vinci by practicing creative thinking or by silencing mental noise. But creativity can be improved significantly within the same individual, sliding with SoM.

What we have learned so far is that reducing mental load, stress, and ruminations is one powerful means for amplifying one's creative abilities. But an equally important point in this context is that being creative is our default state, and it's the same with being exploratory and curious; we are born that way. Mindwandering can be a waste of time, or it can be a fountain of creativity and exploration, and it all depends on our state of mind.

Creativity and Curiosity

Creativity and curiosity can be seen as two sides of the same entity. In creativity, we generate something that is novel and useful in some way. In curiosity, we orient our attention with the intention of gathering information—not formal definitions, because there are none that are widely accepted and we do not really need any for now. Creativity is like a transmission process, whereby we generate ideas, solutions, and thoughts and transmit them to the world. This is done not necessarily verbally or even explicitly, but they are generated by us with some kind of "outward" relevance, such as for action. Curiosity, on the other end, is an act of receiving. We consume the world, taking in information for internal purposes. But while one is inward oriented and the other outward oriented, they are synchronized because they are mediated by overlapping mechanisms. Highly creative is highly curious, and vice versa. Both are based on motivation to seek information: in curiosity it is clear, and in creativity the motivation for information is more metaphorical in that our neurons go far to seek an original solution. Creativity and curiosity are affected similarly by load and by freedom of thought: mental availability is critical for both, and a broad scope of thought and perception is conducive for both. The good news is that our mind wants to be in a state of creativity and curiosity by default. The less good news is that our life interferes with these default characteristics on a regular basis, with our own implicit yet highly effective consent.

The issue of eliminating mental clutter, silencing background thoughts, and focusing on what is important brings back the issue of observing thoughts, this time in the context of creativity and curiosity. Unlike the stream-of-consciousness type of thoughts, of which we are fully aware, and sometimes can even control to some extent, we are not as privy to what goes on in our mind during either the creative process or the state of being curious about something. They are both primarily below the level of our conscious awareness. Before an insight solution strikes us, an aha! moment, we do not have much access to what is going on. We can try to observe the underlying incubation for as long as we want, but we will not be able to because it is obscured from our conscious mind by design. So not all thoughts are observable. It is even hard for us to talk about our own creative process after the fact. And that's true not only for us. I recently watched an interview with one of the most creative film directors, of whom I am a huge fan, and he was asked to describe how he arrives at all those original, bizarre ideas that are so characteristic of his movies. It was a sad response to watch; he was evidently struggling to say something insightful about what is going through his mind before a creative thought comes around, to no avail. It was no wonder; we are not exposed to the process, and we are left with the heroic desire still to explain.

Inhibition and Mental Progression

Constructive mindwandering, a creative mind, and a happy mood all rely on the same single characteristic: *ease of mental progression*. Our thoughts need to be broad, go far, and advance fast, which together max-imizes how much semantic ground is covered by our mind. This is the opposite of ruminative thinking. We want mental movement to be effi-cient. The smoother, the merrier, but not more; our thought process still needs to be contained. This is where inhibition comes in.

For most of us cognitive neuroscientists, it is more intuitive to think about excitation in the brain than about inhibition, that the operation of the brain is achieved via the excitation of neurons, circuits, represen-tations, concepts, words, numbers, emotions, motor movements, and thoughts. Excitation sounds equivalent to activation, whereas inhibition gives the impression of resistance, dampening, diminishing—much less exciting. But the truth is that inhibition is as important and as construc-tive as excitation; it is a force for pruning, for curbing, and for regulating. It is the balance between excitation and inhibition that counts. Here is one example.

Over the course of our lifetime we learn many associations in our world: that pillows are usually found on beds, that smoking is unhealthy, that snakes are dangerous, that grapes make wine, that coffee often comes with milk, and that where there is a chair there is usually also a table. The brain picks up these statistical regularities and represents them as such. So, a chair is connected to a table, pillow to a bed, and headphones to heads, and these connections are probabilistic. Not every bed has a pillow on it, perhaps only 85 percent of those that we have encountered; likewise, not all headphones we have seen appeared on heads, perhaps only 40 percent. The probability of such co-occurrences determines the strength of their connection in the brain, and the strength of their connection determines the likelihood of their coactivation; when one is activated, so is the other. These coactivations are the predictions of what to expect to encounter in that scene. When you know you are about to enter a kitchen, you expect to see a sink and a stove in very high probability, a coffee maker in lower probability, and a waffle maker in an even lower (but still possible) probability. Things that you do not expect based on your experience, such as a samurai sword, would surprise you, not to say startle, and will cause confusion. Confusions and, more generally, surprises lead to learning and updating our representations of what is possible in specific contexts. The next time you see a samurai sword in a kitchen, it will be much less surprising . . .

Now let's consider the associations of the associates. A pillow leads you to think of bed, and a bed, in turn, is associated with linens, linens with cotton, cotton with cotton fields, and cotton fields for you are associated with Creedence Clearwater Revival. You do not want to think of Creedence Clearwater Revival every time you see a pillow; it is not relevant in the specific context, it expends unnecessary neuronal energy that will be required for this superfluous activation, and it will mislead you to search for relevance when there is none. Something has to tell your brain not to activate associations that are too remote and irrelevant, and that something is inhibition. We want our brains to be associative but not overly associative, to be excited but only to the extent that it is helpful. So, when you see an object in your environment, there is some tug-of-war taking place in your brain between exciting and inhibiting associations, and the result, typically, is that only the relevant associations are activated and are there for you as predictions.

There are some intriguing exceptions to this. Consider, for example, words such as "blow," "stick," "shot," "crush," "bank," "bear," and "cut." They are all homonyms with multiple meanings ("cut" has seventy different meanings, according to some estimates). Your brain does not know what other associations to activate with such homonyms because it depends on the specific meaning of that word in that instance, which is often disambiguated with context information (bear with me . . .). Until the relevant meaning is disambiguated, irrelevant associations will be initially activated and only later inhibited.

It is also interesting to consider cases where high inhibition is desirable and cases when lower inhibition is better. Keeping secrets relies on inhibition, as does self-control when avoiding saying unintended or inappropriate things. It's like those court scenes in movies where the witness on the stand is under attack from the prosecutor and breaks down and confesses, or like a poor young faculty member at our research center who recently during his first talk in front of a large audience, clearly nervous, said something so inappropriate that he then had to apologize broadly, and we all had to have a workplace ethics workshop as a result. Stress, like cognitive load, consumes the resources needed for inhibition. Indeed, applying mental pressure, such as time pressure to respond very quickly (we call this "response deadline" in the lab), is like adding cognitive load that takes away from the global resources. In cases of nervousness and stress, inhibition is depleted, because the resources required to maintain it have been diverted and are now consumed by stress and load, and our retrieval from memory, as well as our choice of behavior, remains less shielded by the usual checks and balances, and thus more vulnerable for unwanted bypasses.

On the other end of this spectrum, there are cases where we want as little inhibition as possible, particularly in promoting creativity and curiosity; there the uninhibited activation of remote associations and connections is much desirable. You similarly do not want to be inhibited when you explore and prefer to maintain high levels of curiosity. Accordingly, the brain has mechanisms to regulate levels of inhibition and its balance with excitation, that is, how much to apply from each. Nevertheless, this balance can be disrupted in various conditions. Depression, manic behavior, sleep deprivation, and euphoria all entail altered levels of inhibition. Inhibition could also be reduced with alcohol and other drugs, though the dosage is tricky and the change is for the short term.

Last weekend I went to pick up my son, Naor, from a party. He is a serious guy, a soldier, and generally has better composure and self-control than his father. When he got in the car, it was evident that he had had too much to drink at the party. As I was preparing to give him a belated speech about alcohol and reckless behavior, it struck me how giddy and funny he was, making his sisters in the backseat so happy, so I didn't interrupt. Less inhibition leads to better mood—in moderation.

A highly intuitive theory is that when we grow up, society imposes more and more inhibitions on our behavior, making us not only civilized but also less creative and often less happy—the Victorian suppresses the Bohemian, in Ernest Schachtel's words.[4]

Inhibition comes from all kind of places and processes in the brain, but one major region that is associated with inhibition is the prefrontal cortex. Inhibition is essential for control and other executive decisions the brain ought to make, as well as for mood regulation. The prefrontal cortex is the area of the human brain that is, by far, the latest to mature, around the midtwenties. One does not need an elaborate experiment, or even to be a neuroscientist, to notice that children, whose prefrontal cortex is yet to be developed, are typically more creative, more curious, less inhibited (as in telling you the truth to your face or making new friends very quickly), more impulsive, more exploratory, and in a better mood. Like the late and talented Vic Chesnutt says in the song "Parade": "Everybody over ten years old is frowning."

ADHD is also relevant here. Attention is guided, restricted, and maintained using control signals. These signals are also composed of a combination of excitation and inhibition: attend these areas of the visual scene, but not those. If we think of the scope of attention as a spotlight, what is inside that spotlight is enhanced through excitation, and what is outside the spotlight is suppressed through inhibition. In ADHD, because of reduced inhibition, the borders of this spotlight are not as rigid; it is closer to the "diffused attention" they have been trying to teach me to achieve in meditation retreats, and the result is a mixed blessing. Individuals with ADHD are easily distracted, less focused, and more impulsive, but also more creative, often in a better mood, and more curious.

The same element that is required to control and guide attention and to generate properly pruned predictions is what makes us less creative, less curious, and less exploratory.

Boredom, Idle Minds, and Wandering Minds

One of the best perks of having lived for a while already, and having gained sufficient confidence over the years, is that I hardly let myself suffer boredom anymore. Any meeting, social gathering, or other situation where I feel that all-encompassing boredom-induced fatigue in my body, I stand up and leave. And when I can't, I experiment with my mind.

Boredom is an annoying yet highly enigmatic emotion. A state of boredom always feels long, wasteful, and useless. Why it is so unbearable is fascinating. I started thinking about boredom in earnest right after my first weeklong silence retreat. I realized I am beside myself when I am stuck in traffic or need to wait in a slow line, in striking contrast to the week before, in the retreat, where I could sit on a bench for long minutes calmly doing nothing while waiting for dinner. Is it just the difference in context and state of mind that makes idle time feel like either death or bliss? It has to be more than that. In weeklong retreats of silence and meditation, we are able to stare at ants on the ground for eternity because the senses have opened up. Staring provides you with enough stimulation; you do not need to go anywhere when the senses are so sensitive, and everything suddenly looks so interesting.

Outside the comparison between retreats and the real world, it is curious why at times an interval of nothingness could be the launching pad for great creative ideas and at other times your mind seems to be empty with only one thought: "When will this end, for crying out loud?" There are various possible explanations for why boredom feels the way it does, from impatient personality to existential accounts connecting the feeling of boredom with the fact that people usually do not want to face their thoughts and would do anything to escape themselves. In some experiments it was even reported that people would rather give themselves small electric shocks than just sit quietly in front of a white wall.[5] Boredom feels like mental pain.

When we are bored we feel that time hardly passes, which is also the case when we suffer. It is a strange state: we do not do anything, yet our mind seems full; we ruminate on nothingness. What is more, pure boredom kills curiosity and creativity. This is intriguing because we know we need an empty and available mind to be creative and have room for curiosity. This is one of those puzzles we scientists like to encounter because they open up new grounds for new understandings. So, some emptiness of mind breeds creativity and curiosity, and some emptiness is unbearably annoying; characterizing the difference is sure to yield something interesting. The idleness that Bertrand Russell praised cannot be the one that makes us bored.

Distinguishing types of emptiness is directly related to our drive for understanding the effect of thought and our inner world on the quality of experience.[6] Roughly speaking, there are three possible states of idleness: doing nothing and being bored (with individually varying levels of tolerance to this state); doing nothing but being calm and relaxed about it, like at a meditation retreat or on the beach on a vacation; or doing nothing but mindwandering extensively and having creative and constructive thoughts. What is really of interest is that some idleness situations allow and are even conducive to mindwandering, but in other states, even in a very similar situation, your mind is not as crafty, and even if you tell yourself, "Okay, I'm stuck here, so I might as well daydream in the meantime or fantasize about something fun," it does not work.

At first it may seem that we prefer to mindwander only when it comes at the expense of something else we need to be doing, some sort of an escape from the moment. But the real explanation is that mindwandering is controlled beyond our conscious reach, so the mind will wander by need regardless, assuming the resources are available. This supports the notion that mindwandering serves a function, and it is not subjected to our voluntary control of when to wander or where to wander. That we cannot mindwander by conscious decision is also why it is so hard to stop mindwandering at will. We cannot start and we cannot stop mindwandering voluntarily.

What we can do, instead, is understand how the subconscious decides for us to mindwander or not, why, and when. In mindfulness meditation we actually try, indirectly, to take control over the operation of the subconscious. We make it stop sending us to wander. The way we do it is not forcefully, but gently. The subconscious mind sends us wandering, via our conscious mind, about a certain thought; we embrace this conscious thought and move on. We refuse to fight it but rather accept it and observe it instead. After we let it go, be it through labeling or anything else, the subconscious sends the next thought, and the same thing happens. Thus, to empty our mind, what we actually do is empty our subconscious mind, until there is nothing for it to send us wandering to. The opposite—making ourselves mindwander at will when we seek new ideas or just mental entertainment to replace a boring situation—you now know, requires no task and a positive mood.

Habits of the Mind

Just as habits of behavior "die hard," so do habits of the mind. Habits are a double-edged sword. On the one hand, they are an ingenious mechanism that evolution has instilled in us to automatize our interactions, thereby saving us time and helping us survive better. You learn something for the first time, and then you get to do it again, and again, and again, learning from your mistakes, learning what feels best for you, and at some point you perfect it. Then your brain starts delegating this skill, or habit, from your conscious mind, which initially required much deliberation and attention for every step, to your more automatic subconscious mind, which can do the exact same thing without bothering the conscious you. This skill is now said to be automatic, which is a habit, like a mental autopilot, freeing your mind for other things, such as acquiring new experiences.

Those things that you learn and practice and then outsource can be, for example, how to make an omelet and how to drive a car, how to recognize a risky situation, and how to plan your escape route from a boring gathering. It can also help you "jump" to conclusions. Autopiloting how to drive means not thinking about the physical and attentional operations required to drive safely. You just do it, which explains why we all tend to forget long stretches of our daily commute because our mind was not part of the process and therefore wandered off and did not pay attention to what the subconscious mind took care of in the background. Mental autopiloting, similarly, means performing mental operations without consciously thinking about them too much. A good analogy is solving simple multiplications from the multiplication table. As a young child, you had to work hard to answer when your teacher asked how much is eight times nine because you actually calculated it. Gradually, the response becomes automatic. You just say seventy-two without thinking. This is not much of a delegation to the subconscious as it is an associative mental shortcut to bring you straight to the final answer based on your experience. The neural path that used to lead you to the answer as a child has been replaced by a direct connection.

More complex mental challenges can also be solved without thinking but based on operations that are done in the background because they have become automatic with experience, which we sometimes call "intuition." In fact, as a kid gifted in math, it can get really frustrating if a teacher asks you how you reached the correct answer and you just cannot reconstruct your correct intuition. You would need to reverse engineer a solution to satisfy your teacher. But perhaps the most notorious of mental habits is quick and superficial judgment.

They say first impressions are lasting impressions for a reason; it is simply very hard to change them. It is one thing if those impressions were accurate, veridical, but they are not. We generate impressions of people blazingly fast, based on superficial information, and then we hold on to them for a long time even in the face of counterevidence. The brain has evolved to take advantage of statistical regularities, those aspects of our environment that tend to repeat in similar ways. We know that a conference room will contain chairs, that a party will likely have drinks, that you need to dress nicely when going to the opera, what strawberry jam tastes like, and what various uses for a knife are. This is a good thing. Imagine you had to relearn the concept of a chair each time you saw a new chair. Life would take forever. Instead, when encountering something we have not encountered before, the brain asks, "What is this like?" You connect that new chair to the category of chairs you already have in memory, and then immediately gain access to vast amounts of associations and knowledge. You know what its function is and how it would feel to use it, you can imagine it in various situations, you can predict what other objects tend to appear with it, and so on.

This is marvelous, powerful, and very useful. But it is far from being desired when it comes to our interactions with people. When a new person you meet reminds you of someone else, you do not want to project all the traits and memories and attitudes you have from that old friend onto that new person, but you do. We are all different individuals, and it has already been shown that we are really bad at guessing what kind of a person that new someone is in reality, but we keep on doing it, out of habit. What is good habit for objects and situations is not good when it comes to judging our fellow humans with no information.

I rented a shack in the gorgeous North of Israel (Clil in the Galil) for a couple of months to work on this book—nature, chickens, and no cell-phone reception. For the first payment I really had to nudge the hippie landlord to take my check. The impression was that he was very relaxed overall and certainly not concerned with money. Taking this into account on some level, I also became relaxed about paying for the next month . . . , to the point that I had not taken his requests too seriously and it took several reminders for me to understand he really wanted me to pay. My first impression of his attitude toward money was swift and then rigid. I had formed a template, as we all do, from a single encounter, and this quick first impression could not be updated easily, even in the face of repeated counterexamples.

Our habit for swift impressions not only is unfair and harmful in interactions, but also robs us of the exquisite pleasure of enjoying things afresh. Walter Pater, in the stunning conclusion of his book *The Renaissance: Studies in Art and Poetry*, says:

> The service of philosophy, of speculative culture, towards the human spirit, is to rouse, to startle it to a life of constant and eager observation. Every moment some form grows perfect in hand or face; some tone on the hills or the sea is choicer than the rest; some

mood of passion or insight or intellectual excitement is irresistibly real and attractive to us,—for that moment only. Not the fruit of experience, but experience itself, is the end. A counted number of pulses only is given to us of a variegated, dramatic life. How may we see in them all that is to be seen in them by the finest senses? How shall we pass most swiftly from point to point, and be present always at the focus where the greatest number of vital forces unite in their purest energy?

To burn always with this hard, gemlike flame, to maintain this ecstasy, is success in life. In a sense it might even be said that our failure is to form habits: for, after all, habit is relative to a stereotyped world, and meantime it is only the roughness of the eye that makes any two persons, things, situations, seem alike.

Our failure is to form habits, he says.

No moment in life is like another moment, no person is like another person, no flower is like another flower, and every sunset is different. The same awesome habitual mechanism of the brain and mind that saves us processing resources by finding quick "what is this like" analogies for objects, is the mechanism that makes us see individuals as categories, and the same mechanism that prevents us from enjoying an éclair as richly every time we have one.

Scientists know that great breakthroughs require abandoning prejudices and old assumptions. This is like looking at the world afresh, quitting expectations and top-down. This is why newcomers should be encouraged to speak their mind; they are a great source for unmounting the fixated expert mind. Getting back to our old self is the easiest thing to do. This is why people like Zen authority Shunryu Suzuki advocate that all of us strive to nurture *a beginner's mind*. An expert's mind is fixed and rigid (though expert nevertheless . . .), but a beginner's mind leaves many possibilities open.

Personality traits are also habits, broadly defined. We can think of personality as one big bag of habits (and dispositions), like states of mind but much more firm and permanent. Traits are the most hard-wired habits of them all; can one easily stop being an introvert or open for new experiences? Desires and obsessions can also be seen as habits of thought, and we know how hard these can be to get rid of. One more interesting type of mental habit is superstitious beliefs and magical thinking, the tendency to see relationships, causality, and effects where there are none. Just like it is difficult to start a diet, go to the gym regularly, quit smoking, or relinquish your cell phone, it is hard to quit those engrained habits of the mind.

Mindwandering is also a mind habit. It seems that our proclivity for mental movement cannot be stopped. The difficulty that new as well as experienced meditators encounter is the clearest manifestation of how hard it is to break a mental habit. The mind wants to be busy. When you are done with what was on your mind, this drive for mental busy-ness fills you with new, even mundane stuff, like useless details about strangers around you. You feel it in retreats. When done with the tons of thoughts with which I came to the retreat, my mind then fills with more local little thoughts of the current context—the bag of the girl in front of me, the tattoo of the guy to my right. Sit and think of nothing—how hard can it be? Imagine telling a hyperactive kid to sit still, when not only his hyperactivity drives him to move but his entire environment is filled with stimulating objects, candies, and toys that are calling him to rumble.

IN SUM: FIVE POINTS TO KEEP IN MIND

THE FIRST POINT IS THAT IF YOUR MIND WANDERS—AND WHEN DOES IT not?—mind the ease of mental progression. For better mood and for better ideas, it is best to wander broadly, far, and fast.

The second is that our mindwandering is awesome in yet another way: it is a tool that allows us to learn from imagined experiences. We can facilitate decisions and possible future experiences by simply fabricating them in advance.

The third is that our mind has different states. These states are dynamic and cluster together the many aspects of our mental being: perception, attention, thought, openness, and mood. There is a right mind for the right occasion, and our mission is to maximize the match and minimize the friction.

The fourth is that we should meditate, if only to better understand our thoughts and the different qualities of our experience.

The fifth is immersion. To go back to Walter Pater, *"Not the fruit of experience, but experience itself, is the end."*

Appendix: From the Lab to Everyday Life

MOST OF MY RESEARCH IDEAS, FINDINGS, AND THEORIES OVER MANY years in science were triggered by little things around my life that had attracted my curiosity, seemed odd, or just begged to be explained and generalized. It gives me great pleasure to bring those fruits back full circle with the aim of being relevant and applicable outside the lab. Some of them are listed here with examples, most from my own experience, and some are highlighted excerpts from the text. They are provided here so that you may consider them as you move on. Enjoy.

Intentional Wandering

Mindwandering is a major activity in the brain. While it is not always welcomed, such as when we really need to be accomplishing something else, or when it sends us ruminating and thus dampens our mood, in the right context it is a precious resource. We should not feel guilty when we catch ourselves wandering; it could be an inventive habit that is worth deliberately allocating time for. Once we do, we should get the most out of it.

Learning from simulated experiences. A great deal of what we have in memory is a result of actual experience, but some of it is also the outcome of imagined experiences and simulated scenarios. It is magnificent that we do not have to experience in order to learn. I would have recommended to commit those imagined scenarios to memory, but it happens anyhow. My research into the possibility that our brain also stores memories of imagined experiences although they have never taken place started a while ago on a flight. I was reviewing a paper, and my mind drifted until it landed on the emergency door, which triggered the following simulation: What if the door suddenly opens while we are in the air? I will need a parachute; I could probably use the airplane blanket on my lap; but I will not be able to hold on to it in the strong wind—it needs holes; I can use my pen for making the holes; and so on. Far-fetched, funny every time, but nevertheless I now have a script of an imagined experience stored in memory, and it would be helpful should the unlikely event ever take place. We do this often, in much likelier situations.

Semidirected mindwandering. While we cannot really tell our mind what to wander about, we can strive to fill the mental space of possibilities with content that we would have liked to be wandering about, either because we seek new ideas or because it makes us feel good, or both. Before I go on a long walk, or any other activity that is not overly demanding, I ask myself what is on my mind. If it is something like the bills I just paid or an annoying email, I try to replace it with something that I'd rather be spending my mindwandering stretch on instead, such as rereading a paragraph that caught my interest recently. Or I might bring back a problem that engaged me before I gave up on it or warm up the idea of an upcoming trip so that I can fine-tune the details as I simulate the future with my mind.

The conditions that invite constructive mindwandering. The most creative and uplifting mindwandering requires that we will have no demanding task to accomplish, coupled with a positive mood.

Wander Broad, Far, and Fast for Mood and Creativity

Ease of mental progression. Constructive mindwandering, a creative mind, and a happy mood all rely on the same single characteristic: *ease of mental progression*. Our thoughts need to be broad, go far, and advance fast, which together maximizes how much semantic ground is covered by our thoughts. This is the opposite of ruminative thinking. We want mental movement to be efficient: the smoother, the merrier, but not more; our thought process still needs to be contained. Now that I am aware of that, I make a regular effort to identify my own obstacles.

Broad thinking. How we think can affect how we feel. The pattern of thinking, independent of its content, can directly influence our mood. It has been known for a while that the other direction of influence exists: how we feel affects how we think. People in a good mood tend to be more creative, better at solving problems that require insight and "aha!" solutions, and have access to more unusual information in memory than people in a negative mood. More important to our well-being, however, is the opposite direction, the potential to improve mood by changing thought patterns. Chronic ruminations are not easily diminished, even if we now understand how they work. But for less severe ruminations, we need to remember that associative thinking that progresses broadly is conducive for a better mood. Some examples of associative chains that broadened our participants' thinking and improved their mood:

> towel–robe–king–queen–England–clock–bell–church–cross–
> cemetery–tomb–flowers

> tomato–red–blood–knife–fork–spoon–silver–coin–quarter–
> parking–meter–ticket–cop

> tent–circus–elephant–peanut–peanut butter–jelly–donut–hole–
> shovel–rake–leaf–branch

> television–book–shelf–closet–jacket–gloves–hat–cap–baseball–
> bat–cave–bear

> teeth–tongue–muscle–barbell–sneakers–feet–toes–nail–polish–
> cotton–cloud–bird–airplane

While there isn't much content that we can enforce on our thinking, we can change the way it flows. We can observe our thought pattern and first see if it is ruminative. If it is, a healthy distraction could work, as well as thought labeling. Even when we do not ruminate, we may prefer broader thinking for better and more original ideas. Start by making broad lists of your own, and this will already expand your thinking.

Better mood through a manic-like thinking style. Another surprisingly simple method for improving mood is by reading text exceptionally rapidly. Read a text of your choice as fast as you can. It still needs to be understandable, but exhilarating at the same time. Reading fast induces a manic-like state, which is known to involve elation and exhilaration. Indeed, after reading fast, participants showed other characteristics of mania, such as a subjective feeling of power, creativity, and a sense of increased energy. Maybe you'll be as lucky.

Minimized inhibition. Inhibition is the mechanism that limits the speed, scope, and distance of our thoughts. A more inhibited person will more likely suffer from mood disorders, while a less inhibited person will be more creative, to put it somewhat simplistically. When there is less inhibition, there is less stagnation. Meditation is proven for some already as helpful in shutting off such inhibitory top-down influences. So is immersion. Otherwise, the search for the environments and contexts that are fitted for your own release of inhibitions is a personal one, and you could find yours.

Reduced cognitive load. Multiple sources can simultaneously tax brain processes and our mental availability. If you walk the aisles of a supermarket with two crying toddlers, you will not be able to explore or even notice new products on the shelves. Being mentally loaded reduces creativity, and it implies a closed, narrow state of mind, with narrow (local) perception and attention, narrow thinking and a less positive mood, and in an overall exploitatory state. Reducing cognitive load increases creativity and makes one more exploratory, broadens perceptual and mental scope, and improves mood. Of course, we do not always have the luxury of escaping cognitive load with the practicalities of our everyday demands, but even then, recognizing our limited state will help in directing us to the activities most appropriate for that state.

States of Mind

Our state of mind is overarching in that it encompasses the pillars of our mental life: perception, attention, thought, openness, and mood. As such, we have multiple "entry points" through which we can manipulate our SoM to be optimal for the specific context. In different situations, each of these can be more or less accessible for changes.

There are a number of means that I have found helpful in calibrating my mental state, some of which we use in my lab and others that I've been working into my life, which I've found quite enriching. Whether we are more broad and open in our SoM or more narrow and closed can be manipulated through any of the entry points, depending on what's available in the specific context. Perception and attention can both be more global (seeing and attending the "forest") or more local (seeing and attending the "trees"). You can start by examining the global aspects of pictures to make your SoM broader, or scrutinize the little details instead and your SoM will gradually become narrower. Thinking can also help change our SoM to be broader or narrower, per the methods already suggested above. Openness, tolerance for uncertainty, or being more exploratory or more exploitatory can similarly be changed and consequently change our SoM. Seeking new environments to explore, trying a new dish, or seeking most other things that make you uncomfortable might help change your attitude toward temporary uncertainty and novelty. Finally, mood can also be manipulated in some contexts, even if just superficially and for a short duration; sometimes just ice cream and a funny movie can do the trick. Changing any of these will change the others correspondingly, and together they can help us bring our overarching SoM closer to where we want it to be.

Time of day is another factor in determining where we are on the exploration-exploitation spectrum. While we dread any changes to our morning coffee, most of us are open for a surprise dish by lunchtime. This is, of course, individual, and by being aware you can experiment and understand your own correlation between SoM and time of day.

Becoming familiar with ways of gauging your state of mind can help you optimize activities per state. Mindfulness meditation, for example, is of great help with staying aware that we should be monitoring our mental state. States of mind, and their manipulation, can be harnessed for better performance. When you are in a happy mood, it is hard to sit still, and thus it is not the best state for a boring chore, and it is also good to know that when you are in this state, decisions you'll make will tend to be riskier. It is, however, the best state for coming up with a nonconventional solution for a problem. Your best state for exploring new territories without anxiety is the state of broadly associative thinking, and vice versa, because all these codependencies within our SoM are reciprocal.

When I am in a broad and open SoM, I allow myself to stay upbeat and seek out some exploratory activity to take advantage of that mood, or I let my mind wander in hopes of coming up with some good new ideas to pursue in my work. I've started respecting my spontaneous bursts of mindwandering. If my wandering is becoming ruminative, though, I am usually able to do something to break the spell. One way I do so is by seeking a quick immersive distraction. Over time, taking a state-of-mind check becomes second nature. I now make a conscious observation of my mental state during any experience, when I remember, and decide whether I want to observe myself experiencing it, as I do in my beginner's yoga class so I can improve, or want to immerse in it as much as I can.

Top-down or bottom-up? State of mind is shaped by the ratio between top-down and bottom-up influences. Now that we know that top-down influences come from memory and previous experience while bottom-up influences come from the current environment as conveyed by our senses, we can use it to our advantage. Not that we have perfect control over what influences us, but we can strive to remain minded of those differences such that if we're on a vacation with our kids, a date with our lover, eating a mango, or viewing art, we will try to be more attuned to the bottom-up signals while working to silence the old signals from within. On the other hand, if we want to lean on the familiar for efficiency and for certainty, we should try to give more emphasis to our inner knowledge. And if we're searching for a big new idea—say, for a product to create—we want to be in broadly associative mindwandering mode. I've been much better able to immerse myself in the experience of spending time with Nili and my two older children, Nadia and Naor, though it is never enough.

Tolerance for uncertainty. We categorize in order to have meaning and thus feel some subjective certainty that we know what is going on and that we are in control. Not feeling pressure to fit new things into old templates requires being able to tolerate uncertainty. Tolerance for uncertainty comes in an exploratory state of mind, where one is open, curious, broad, creative, and in a good mood, just like kids, who, luckily for them, indeed do not care much about borders. Borders, rules, and categories come from the prefrontal cortex, which they have not developed yet. For us to emulate this state we need to find a way to give in to our senses.

A window for change. The window of opportunity to influence our first impressions is extremely brief. In new situations we first open the exploratory window briefly so that we can learn and create a new template, and then it is both stable and rigid. Very quickly, we turn back to our default state of exploitation, leaning on what that swift window of exploration has imprinted on us. Awareness of this somewhat frustrating fact is key here. Fighting these biases when they are not founded is far from trivial, but realizing that we are going far in our judgment based on very little is something that we should not forget.

Immerse Yourself

Immersion is a different way of experiencing, which requires a radical change of perspective, not thinking, not wandering, not observing ourselves, and not expecting anything, just sensing.

I can't recommend more vigorously that we should all regularly make some time in our lives for immersive experiences. Ask yourself when the last time was that you were so engaged in an activity that you got truly lost in it. Schedule some time to give yourself the luxury of that experience again or some other deeply consuming experience. Search for some new ones. Have you wondered why anyone would pay good money to zip-line over a mountain chasm? Well, give it a whirl. Have you tried the crazy Vegas roller coaster strapped into an augmented reality helmet that simulates an alien attack on Vegas yet? Being engrossed in our work is, of course, the most clearly productive form of immersion, but these other experiences are far from frivolous. Once you practice immersion in intense adventures, you will gradually be able to apply this immersive skill also in less thrilling situations, thereby making them more thrilling than they used to seem.

I wish I could say we know what conditions summon spontaneous immersion, but the psychological and neuroscientific studies on that are just beginning. What I can attest to, though, is that we can voluntarily immerse ourselves "on demand" to a great extent. My favorite consciously immersive experiences are the ones I have with my children. I put my phone aside, lean forward, open my eyes and ears widely, and sink in. It is a sort of mini meditation I've honed for myself, where instead of focusing on my breath and returning to it when my mind drifts, I am focusing on my children. I never thought I could feel so elated playing with Barbies or making sandwiches together. Unfortunately, this does not happen often enough. Of course, we can't be busy all day focusing on our state of mind, but we can learn to remind ourselves to do it much more often.

Meditate on Your Thoughts

This is not a call to meditate; it works for me and possibly also would for you, but it is not a must. Meditation is brought here and throughout the book for the principles it offers, which could be implemented in an intuitive, though not necessarily easy, way in our lives.

There are three components that can explain the power of meditation to foster a mindful life. The first is *diffused attention*: the ability to attend your environment with equal weight to all locations and all items surrounding you, with no bias and no privileged allocation. This is certainly not always desired. When you are looking for your car keys, your friend in a crowd, or the hockey puck, you want your attentional spotlight to be very specific, with information about both possible locations and possible features. Think "Where's Waldo?" But when we are not in need of finding anything in particular, and we have the luxury of surveying the scene around us, in those times we not only want to broaden our attentional spotlight, but would rather have no spotlight at all. All parts of our environment have the potential of being interesting, and when we can, we want to be open to receive.

The second thing that meditation does to your brain to make it mindful is to *turn off expectations*. The default state of our brain is to expect: to expect something to happen, to expect something to be good or bad, to want something in the future, and to judge things in relation to how they fare compared with our anticipation. Watching your on-going breath is the trick that makes you be here and now by gradually diminishing the involvement of top-down information. And by being here and now, you are cut off from thinking about the future, which is what expectation is all about. When you expect nothing, you are open to what is coming.

The third component that makes meditation so effective for the quality of present experience is *reducing clinging* to our thoughts, desires, and fears. In my experience, the best approach to fight that is through labeling. While it is a research topic that is still developing in my lab, the method can already be adopted. You examine a specific thought that occupies your mind and label it along a couple of dimensions: Is it positive, negative, or neutral in terms of the emotions that it elicits? Is it about the past, present, or future? Is it about you, others, or both? So, if you think about the sad ending of the movie you watched last night, it will be labeled as negative, past, others. If you think about your daughter's trip away for two months, it will be labeled as negative, future, self. (You can think of other dimensions as well.) You engage in this exercise, and thoughts start to disappear as soon as you finish labeling them. So what if worries float into your mind? You acknowledge them, stick a label on them, and move on.

A beginner's mind. Scientists know that great breakthroughs require abandoning prejudices and old assumptions. This is like looking at the world afresh, quitting expectations and top-down thinking. This is why newcomers should be encouraged to speak their mind; they are a great source for unmounting the fixated expert mind. Getting back to our old self is the easiest thing to do. A beginner's mind leaves many possibilities open.

Sundries

Mental salivation. Make things more plausible by making them appear more plausible through the simulations I call *mental salivation*. You are laying on your sofa and cannot gather the energy to go back to your computer, go shopping, or go to the gym. Start imagining the upcoming activity in detail, of the grocery shopping, for example: the list you've made, the recyclable bags you want to take with you, where you'll park, the aisles you will need to stroll along and how you remember they look, the flowers to pick up on your way out, and the feeling of accomplishment you will feel once you are back home. The whole experience suddenly seems closer, with no buffers and obstacles between you and actually getting off that sofa. (This should not be taken as advice for fighting procrastination more generally. I believe that procrastination often serves a purpose, creative incubation in particular, and as such should not always be fought.)

Abolishing conventions and borders. I told the story of the friend who went to buy flowers, and when the lady told him that those flowers did not go together, he said, "Tie them together and they will." I like to play with borders in my life, weighing the pros and cons of strict versus flexible categorical fences at different intersections where I need to choose between what I want and what is expected. A good lesson from my friend's flower story is that what seems impossible before we encounter it, which means before we could predict it as a possibility, becomes possible once it takes place. "Weird" becomes "normal" when it is familiar.

Alleviating by sharing. Merely sharing a sore thought or a daunting worry is sufficient for alleviating much of the pain it causes. Talking to someone, or even to yourself, as well as simply writing it down on paper surprisingly does the trick for most everyday little concerns.

Considering affordance. To what extent does what is in front of you afford a specific action? This principle can guide design and is applicable in architecture, advertising, product design, and more. When I advise various companies, I emphasize that the design of their product needs to make it easy for a potential customer to see or simulate himself using that product, so they should make it obvious how the intended action is afforded by the design. If it is a washing detergent, make the design help people see themselves actually holding the grip and pouring the detergent. You would want them to imagine that in as much detail as possible, to facilitate the mental salivation from above, for it to be convincing. I do the same also with my kids and with other people when trying to convince them of a certain path: make the steps concrete enough to be simulate-able. The better we can see ourselves in the pondered activity, the more certain we feel and the better positioned we are for a decision. I only wish we could bring peace to the Middle East with proper mental simulations by all sides.

Taken together, the key obstacles for experiencing life to the fullest are top-down dispositions, mental load, and not being immersed. Now you have better tools.

Acknowledgments

TELL THOSE YOU LOVE, THOSE WHO CARE FOR YOU, THOSE WHO INSPIRE you, those who challenge you, those who look up to you, and those who look down on you that you love them, for none of us would be where we are without the souls that surround us, especially me. I am the conduit for those who set their eyes on me.

I will start at the top, our three kids: Naor, Nadia, and Nili. I will know that I am a good writer when I will figure out a way to describe my love for you in words, or what you make me feel, or what you make me be. With you as my foundations, nothing is difficult. Your love, your sensitivity, your demeanor, your creativity, your openness, your understanding, your hugs and kisses are what help me have meaning in my life.

Maria (*pici*), my life partner for more than two decades, and the mother of my kids, you gave me shape, depth, and the ultimate happiness. Since we met at the Weizmann Institute's Math Department, and across the universe that we have conquered, you still are and always will be an angel in my life.

Noa, we connected so deep and so naturally. You pushed me higher, you excited me, and you calmed me. Our love made me want to write the best book possible. How I wish we could smile forever; I'll be Ganesh, and you'll be the most beautiful *chuldonet*.

Professionally, I had mountains of inspiration, from numerous generous teachers. Chief among them are Irving Biederman and Shimon Ullman. They each took me under their wings, at different times, and it feels that a part of me stayed there and never left. In Judaism, and I am sure in other religions as well, a teacher is equivalent to a parent. Both Shimon and Irving gave me all I needed without hesitation and without conditions. Shimon got me into the world of science and remains a tall tower to this day. Irving allowed me to connect with the child in me and remain connected throughout my research. He is the epitome of insatiable curiosity and creativity (and thus also of positive mood). I was also tremendously lucky to be working, for a shorter duration, with Daniel Schacter when I arrived at Harvard for my postdoc. Dan is the master of memory research, and of getting things done.

Among my colleagues, I would like to first single out Dan Gilbert. From the days when I aspired to write op-eds, Dan was generous, patient, and brilliant. That I managed to publish in the *New York Times*, *Boston Globe*, and *Los Angeles Times* was largely thanks to his friendship, personality, and gift. When I struggle with a sentence, to this day, I ask myself what would Dan think about it. Thank you, Dan, I'll be there for your next award.

By providing me with an environment of constant insights, creativity, generosity, open-mindedness, and limitless opportunities, Irving, Shimon, Dan, and Dan have helped me realize what a lucky person I am for choosing scientific inquiry as my path. That I have the chutzpah to believe that everything can be studied and answered is largely thanks to you.

Whatever I did not learn from my mentors, I learned from my students. I am so fortunate for believing that I should always surround myself with young and eager minds and that I should listen. Elissa Aminoff, Vadim Axelrod, Shira Baror, Jasmine Boshyan, Helen Feigin, Mark Fenske, Kestas Kveraga, Malia Mason, Maital Neta, Matt Panichello, Amitai Shenhav, Kathrine Shepherd, Amir Tal, Cibu Thomas, and Sabrina Trapp, to name a few whose work was most relevant in writing this book: Thank you! Your collaboration and significant contribution have made my body of research what it is. Your optimism, openness, and originality give me energy every single day. Stay students forever, but if you can't, stay with students forever.

I am also indebted to my many collaborators who have completed and elevated me in every conversation, experiment, or paper we wrote together: Lisa Feldman Barrett for her ambition, vision, and emotion; Maurizio Fava for chaperoning me into the magical world of psychiatry; and Noa Herz for her sharp mind, exquisite writing, and authentic character.

You wouldn't be holding this book if it were not for my agent, Katinka Matson, from the Brockman agency. Katinka is one of a kind and much more than an agent, able to hold the hand of a first-time writer from across the ocean, with professional realism combined with warm encouragement and the most efficient touches to guide me from an idea to a book. They say a good friend will help you move, and a real friend will help you move a body. I'm here, Katinka . . .

To my editor, Dan Ambrosio, young and furious, for the most productive and effective editing process, with the right nudges at the right time with the right attitude: I am lucky to have had you as an editor, and here is to many more books.

Emily Loose, surrounded by cats, tea, and good laughs, thank you for superb and illuminating assistance with the book proposal and for your immense talent. We took off so quickly, and I learned from you what I wish many others could.

James Ryerson (Jamie) from the *New York Times*: You picked my proposal to be featured as an op-ed and triggered a fortunate chain reaction. Your razor-sharp edits before publication made me look like I know how to write.

To Oren Harman, brother, my superstar colleague at Bar-Ilan, and the best possible friend: Thank you for bestowing on me your experience and lessons earned from the many luminous books you have written. So glad we are going to continue growing younger together.

To Adi Pundak-Mintz, my dearest friend, for a connection that cannot be described in words, your infinite wisdom, your endless caring, and your stimulating complexities. I love you, brother; you make me feel privileged.

To Nava Levit-Binnun, my dear friend and bright colleague, for introducing me to Vipassana and for agreeing to talk in hiding during silence retreats.

To the people at Tovana, the Israeli Vipassana organization, who welcomed me with open arms, open minds, and open hearts, Lila Kimhi, Christopher Titmuss, and Stephen Fulder in particular: you remain with me anywhere I go.

To Froggy, for stimulating dormant parts of my cortex and of my heart. You are always beautiful.

To Cactus, you are my constant reminder. Thank you for helping me find an alternative pulse.

To Ami, for making me run on the beautiful beach in between paragraphs, and for proving that one can find a lifelong friend while picking up the kids from kindergarten.

Thank you, Sasha, for ever-surprising space between thoughts. You are the star of Jaffa and beyond.

Sami Sagol, with his Hollywood-material life story and contribution, for encouraging and inspiring me in so many ways: thank you, Sami and family.

To Harvard University, Massachusetts General Hospital, and Bar-Ilan University, thank you for providing me with a home and the best atmosphere for pursuing my ideas and passions.

Special thanks to Einav Sudai and Tsafrir Greenberg for managing my lab. You are a treasure.

To Craig Wynett, the ultimate chief creative officer.

Josh Wachman, thank you for that fantastic Pater reference.

My extended family is what should appear next to the definition of "family" in the dictionary: loving, bonded, challenging, and can hold their liquor. My mother, Hila, well, can there be a book long enough for describing your love for your mother? Smooch, Mama. My father, Avi, is my role model in so many domains and an island of stability for all of us. My sisters, Efrat and Inbal, for showing how charming attention disorder can be, and for a hug that never stops. My young brother, Navot, you are Everest. The Ben-Hamo clan, I love you from here to eternity. I also love and thank Michael and Anna Lando, my forever in-laws, for being exactly who you are.

My late grandpa Itzhak and grandma Michal, thank you for showing how far the warm rays of love can reach.

Pop Smoke (welcome to the party), Lil Peep (she's the one with the broken smile), and Mac Miller (I like my music real loud): you've been a most invigorating soundtrack for this book, and I am sad you could not stay for more.

And, finally, to Mother Nature, you make me happy.

Notes

Introduction

1. See Matthew A. Killingsworth and Daniel T. Gilbert, "A Wandering Mind Is an Unhappy Mind," *Science* (November 12, 2010): 932.

2. Moshe Bar, "Visual Objects in Context," *Nature Reviews Neuroscience* 5 (2004): 617–629, https://doi.org/10.1038/nrn1476.

Chapter 1: Always "On"

1. Marcus E. Raichle, "The Brain's Default Mode Network," *Annual Review of Neuroscience* 38, no. 1 (2015): 433–447.

2. Rotem Botvinik-Nezer et al., "Variability in the Analysis of a Single Neuroimaging Dataset by Many Teams," *Nature* 582 (2020): 84–88, https://doi.org/10.1038/s41586-020-2314-9.

Chapter 2: Connecting with Our Thoughts

1. Marion Milner, *A Life of One's Own* (London: Routledge, 2011).

2. Ulric Neisser and Robert Becklen, "Selective Looking: Attending to Visually Specified Events," *Cognitive Psychology* 7, no. 4 (1975): 480–494.

3. Sarah N. Garfinkel and Hugo D. Critchley, "Threat and the Body: How the Heart Supports Fear Processing," *Trends in Cognitive Sciences* 20, no. 1 (2016): 34–46.

4. Walter A. Brown, "Placebo as a Treatment for Depression," *Neuropsychopharmacology* 10 (1994): 265–269, https://doi.org/10.1038/npp.1994.53.

5. Slavenka Kam-Hansen et al., "Altered Placebo and Drug Labeling Changes the Outcome of Episodic Migraine Attacks," *Science Translational Medicine* 6, no. 218 (2014): 218ra5.

6. Wen Ten et al., "Creativity in Children with ADHD: Effects of Medication and Comparisons with Normal Peers," *Psychiatry Research* 284 (February 2020): https://doi.org/10.1016/j.psychres.2019.112680.

Chapter 3: The Journey from Now

1. See, for example, how interfering with the normal operation of the prefrontal cortex elicits odd outcomes such as becoming inappropriately generous: Leonardo Christov-Moore et al., "Increasing Generosity by Disrupting Prefrontal Cortex," *Social Neuroscience* 12, no. 2 (2017): 174–181, https://doi.org/10.1080/17470919.2016.1154105.

2. Esther H. H. Keulers and Lisa M. Jonkman, "Mind Wandering in Children: Examining Task-Unrelated Thoughts in Computerized Tasks and a Classroom Lesson, and the Association with Different Executive Functions," *Journal of Experimental Child Psychology* 179 (2019): 276–290, https://doi.org/10.1016/j.jecp.2018.11.013.

3. Jerome L. Singer, *The Inner World of Daydreaming* (New York: Harper & Row, 1975).

4. Erin C. Westgate et al., "What Makes Thinking for Pleasure Pleasurable? Emotion," advance online publication (2021), https://doi.org/10.1037/emo0000941.

5. Benjamin Baird et al., "Inspired by Distraction: Mind Wandering Facilitates Creative Incubation," *Psychological Science* 23, no. 10 (2012): 1117–1122, https://doi.org/10.1177/0956797612446024.

6. Malia F. Mason et al., "Wandering Minds: The Default Network and Stimulus-Independent Thought," *Science* 315, no. 5810 (2007): 393–395, https://doi.org/10.1126/science.1131295.

Chapter 4: What Do We Wander About? Our Self First

1. Plutarch, "*Theseus* (23.1)," Internet Classics Archive, http://classics.mit.edu/Plutarch/theseus.html.

2. Christopher G. Davey, Jesus Pujol, and Ben J. Harrison, "Mapping the Self in the Brain's Default Mode Network," *NeuroImage* 132 (2016): 390–397, https://doi.org/10.1016/j.neuroimage.2016.02.022.

3. Silvio Ionta et al., "The Brain Network Reflecting Bodily Self-Consciousness: A Functional Connectivity Study," *Social Cognitive and Affective Neuroscience* 9, no. 12 (2014): 1904–1913, https://doi.org/10.1093/scan/nst185.

4. Aviva Berkovich-Ohana, Joseph Glicksohn, and Abraham Goldstein, "Mindfulness-Induced Changes in Gamma Band Activity: Implications for the Default Mode Network, Self-Reference and Attention," *Clinical Neurophysiology* 123, no. 4 (2012): 700–710, https://doi.org/10.1016/j.clinph.2011.07.048.

5. Ethan Kross, *Chatter: The Voice in Our Head, Why It Matters, and How to Harness It* (New York: Crown, 2021); Charles Fernyhough, *The Voices Within: The History and Science of How We Talk to Ourselves* (New York: Basic Books, 2016); Michael S. Gazzaniga, *Who's in Charge? Free Will and the Science of the Brain* (New York: HarperCollins, 2011).

6. Ben Alderson-Day and Charles Fernyhough, "Inner Speech: Development, Cognitive Functions, Phenomenology, and Neurobiology," *Psychological Bulletin* 141, no. 5 (2015): 931–965, http://dx.doi.org/10.1037/bul0000021.

Chapter 5: This Way Something Potentially Wicked Comes

1. Chet C. Sherwood, Francys Subiaul, and Tadeusz W. Zawidzki, "A Natural History of the Human Mind: Tracing Evolutionary Changes in Brain and Cognition," *Journal of Anatomy* 212, no. 4 (2008): 426–454, https://doi.org/10.1111/j.1469-7580.2008.00868.x; Louise Barrett, Peter Henzi, and Drew Rendall, "Social Brains, Simple Minds: Does Social Complexity Really Require Cognitive Complexity?," *Philosophical Transactions of the Royal Society B Biological Sciences* 362, no. 1480 (2007): 561–575, https://doi.org/10.1098/rstb.2006.1995.

2. Benjamin Baird et al., "Inspired by Distraction: Mind Wandering Facilitates Creative Incubation," *Psychological Science* 23, no. 10 (2012): 1117–1122, https://doi.org/10.1177/0956797612446024.

3. R. Nathan Spreng and Cheryl L. Grady, "Patterns of Brain Activity Supporting Autobiographical Memory, Prospection, and Theory of Mind, and Their Relationship to the Default Mode Network," *Journal of Cognitive Neuroscience* 22, no. 6 (2010): 1112–1123, https://doi.org/10.1162/jocn.2009.2128.

4. Veronica V. Galván, Rosa S. Vessal, and Matthew T. Golley, "The Effects of Cell Phone Conversations on the Attention and Memory of Bystanders," *PLoS One* 8, no. 3 (2013), https://doi.org/10.1371/journal.pone.0058579.

5. Moshe Bar, Maital Neta, and Heather Linz, "Very First Impressions," *Emotion* 6, no. 2 (2006): 269–278, https://doi.org/10.1037/1528-3542.6.2.269.

6. Charles C. Ballew and Alexander Todorov, "Predicting Political Elections from Rapid and Unreflective Face Judgments," *Proceedings of the National Academy of Sciences* 104, no. 46 (2007): 17948–17953, https://doi.org/10.1073/pnas.0705435104.

Chapter 6: Future Memories: Learning from Imagined Experiences

1. Moshe Bar and Shimon Ullman, "Spatial Context in Recognition," *Perception* 25, no. 3 (1996): 343–352, https://doi.org/10.1068/p250343.

2. Moshe Bar et al., "The Units of Thought," *Hippocampus* 17, no. 6 (2007): 420–428.

3. Lien B. Pham and Shelley E. Taylor, "From Thought to Action: Effects of Process- Versus Outcome-Based Mental Simulations on Performance," *Personality and Social Psychology Bulletin* 25, no. 2 (1999): 250–260, https://doi.org/10.1177/0146167299025002010.

4. Sonal Arora et al., "Mental Practice: Effective Stress Management Training for Novice Surgeons," *Journal of the American College of Surgeons* 212, no. 2 (2011): 225–233, https://doi.org/10.1016/j.jamcollsurg.2010.09.025.

5. A. M. Pedersen et al., "Saliva and Gastrointestinal Functions of Taste, Mastication, Swallowing and Digestion," *Oral Diseases* 8, no. 3 (2002): 117–129, https://doi.org/10.1034/j.1601-0825.2002.02851.x.

Chapter 7: The Loss of Novelty

1. Moshe Bar, "The Proactive Brain: Using Analogies and Associations to Generate Predictions," *Trends in Cognitive Sciences* 11, no. 7 (2007): 280–289.

2. David Marr, *Vision: A Computational Investigation into the Human Representation and Processing of Visual Information* (San Francisco: W. H. Freeman, 1982).

3. Moshe Bar, "Visual Objects in Context," *Nature Reviews Neuroscience* 5 (2004): 617–629, https://doi.org/10.1038/nrn1476.

4. R. Schvaneveldt, D. Meyer, and C. Becker, "Lexical Ambiguity, Semantic Context, and Visual Word Recognition," *Journal of Experimental Psychology: Human Perception and Performance* 2, no. 2 (1976): 243–256, https://doi.org/10.1037/0096-1523.2.2.243.

5. Maital Neta and Paul J. Whalen, "The Primacy of Negative Interpretations When Resolving the Valence of Ambiguous Facial Expressions," *Psychological Science* 21, no. 7 (2010): 901–907, https://doi.org/10.1177/0956797610373934.

6. Immanuel Kant, *Prolegomena to Any Future Metaphysics*, trans. James W. Ellington, 2nd ed. (Indianapolis: Hackett, 2001), §32.

7. R. von der Heydt, E. Peterhans, and G. Baumgartner, "Illusory Contours and Cortical Neuron Responses," *Science* 224, no. 4654 (1984): 1260–1262, https://doi.org/10.1126/science.6539501; Benjamin de Haas and Dietrich Samuel Schwarzkopf, "Spatially Selective Responses to Kanizsa and Occlusion Stimuli in Human Visual Cortex," *Scientific Reports* 8, no. 611 (2018), https://doi.org/10.1038/s41598-017-19121-z.

Chapter 8: Templates of Mind and the Limits of Boundaries

1. Andrea J. Stone, *Images from the Underworld: Naj Tunich and the Tradition of Maya Cave Painting* (Austin: University of Texas Press, 1995), 10–11.

2. Alan W. Watts, *The Wisdom of Insecurity: A Message for an Age of Anxiety* (New York: Pantheon Books, 1951), 102.

3. Y. Afiki and M. Bar, "Our Need for Associative Coherence," *Humanities and Social Sciences Communications* 7, no. 80 (2020), https://doi.org/10.1057/s41599-020-00577-w.

4. Moshe Bar and Maital Neta, "Humans Prefer Curved Visual Objects," *Psychological Science* 17, no. 8 (2006): 645–648, https://doi.org/10.1111/j.1467-9280.2006.01759.x.

5. Avishag Shemesh et al., "Affective Response to Architecture: Investigating Human Reaction to Spaces with Different Geometry," *Architectural Science*

Review 60, no. 2 (2017): 116–125, https://doi.org/10.1080/00038628.2016
.1266597.

Chapter 9: Breadth of Thought, Creativity, and Mood

1. Moshe Bar et al., "The Units of Thought," *Hippocampus* 17, no. 6 (2007): 420–428.

2. Eiran Vadim Harel et al., "Linking Major Depression and the Neural Substrates of Associative Processing," *Cognitive, Affective & Behavioral Neuroscience* 16, no. 6 (2016): 1017–1026.

3. Wendy Treynor, Richard Gonzalez, and Susan Nolen-Hoeksema, "Rumination Reconsidered: A Psychometric Analysis," *Cognitive Therapy and Research* 27 (2003): 247–259, https://doi.org/10.1023/A:1023910315561.

4. Shira Baror and Moshe Bar, "Associative Activation and Its Relation to Exploration and Exploitation in the Brain," *Psychological Science* 27, no. 6 (2016): 776–789, https://doi.org/10.1177/0956797616634487.

5. Vadim Axelrod et al., "Increasing Propensity to Mind-Wander with Transcranial Direct Current Stimulation," *Proceedings of the National Academy of Sciences of the United States of America* 112, no. 11 (2015): 3314–3319, https://doi.org/10.1073/pnas.1421435112.

6. Malia F. Mason and Moshe Bar, "The Effect of Mental Progression on Mood," *Journal of Experimental Psychology: General* 141, no. 2 (2012): 217.

7. Emily Pronin and Daniel M. Wegner, "Manic Thinking: Independent Effects of Thought Speed and Thought Content on Mood," *Psychological Science* 17, no. 9 (2006): 807–813, https://doi.org/10.1111/j.1467-9280.2006 .01786.x.

8. P. S. Eriksson et al., "Neurogenesis in the Adult Human Hippocampus," *Nature Medicine* 4 (1998): 1313–1317, https://doi.org/10.1038/3305.

9. Luca Santarelli et al., "Requirement of Hippocampal Neurogenesis for the Behavioral Effects of Antidepressants," *Science* 301, no. 5634 (2003): 805–809; Alexis S. Hill, Amar Sahay, and René Hen, "Increasing Adult Hippocampal Neurogenesis Is Sufficient to Reduce Anxiety and Depression-Like Behaviors," *Neuropsychopharmacology* 40, no. 10 (2015): 2368–2378, https:// doi.org/10.1038/npp.2015.85.

10. Laura Micheli et al., "Depression and Adult Neurogenesis: Positive Effects of the Antidepressant Fluoxetine and of Physical Exercise," *Brain Research Bulletin* 143 (2018): 181–193, https://doi.org/10.1016/j.brainresbull

.2018.09.002; Savita Malhotra and Swapnajeet Sahoo, "Rebuilding the Brain with Psychotherapy," *Indian Journal of Psychiatry* 59, no. 4 (2017): 411–419, https://doi.org/10.4103/0019-5545.217299.

11. Thomas Berger et al., "Adult Hippocampal Neurogenesis in Major Depressive Disorder and Alzheimer's Disease," *Trends in Molecular Medicine* 26, no. 9 (2020): 803–818, https://doi.org/10.1016/j.molmed.2020.03.010.

12. https://jeanlouisnortier.wordpress.com/2020/05/18/word-phrase-of-the -day-with-its-origin-monday-18th-may/.

Chapter 10: Meditation, the Default Brain, and the Quality of Our Experience

1. Britta K. Hölzel et al., "Mindfulness Practice Leads to Increases in Regional Brain Gray Matter Density," *Psychiatry Research* 191, no. 1 (2011): 36–43, https://doi.org/10.1016/j.pscychresns.2010.08.006.

2. Sharon Jones, *Burn After Writing* (New York: Perigree, 2014).

3. Verónica Pérez-Rosas et al., "Deception Detection Using Real-Life Trial Data," *ICMI '15: Proceedings of the 2015 ACM on International Conference on Multimodal Interaction* (November 2015): 59–66.

4. Michael L. Slepian, Jinseok S. Chun, and Malia F. Mason, "The Experience of Secrecy," *Journal of Personality and Social Psychology* 113, no. 1 (2017): 1–33, https://doi.org/10.1037/pspa0000085.

5. Judson A. Brewer et al., "Meditation Experience Is Associated with Differences in Default Mode Network Activity and Connectivity," *Proceedings of the National Academy of Sciences* 108, no. 50 (2011): 20254–20259, https:// doi.org/10.1073/pnas.1112029108.

6. Antoine Lutz et al., "Regulation of the Neural Circuitry of Emotion by Compassion Meditation: Effects of Meditative Expertise," *PLoS One* 3, no. 3 (2008): https://doi.org/10.1371/journal.pone.0001897.

7. Richard J. Davidson et al., "Alterations in Brain and Immune Function Produced by Mindfulness Meditation," *Psychosomatic Medicine* 65, no. 4 (2003): 564–570, https://doi.org/10.1097/01.PSY.0000077505.67574.E3.

Chapter 11: Immersed Living

1. William Blake, *The Marriage of Heaven and Hell* (New York: Dover, 1994), 42.

2. Joseph Glicksohn and Aviva Berkovich-Ohana, "Absorption, Immersion, and Consciousness," in *Video Game Play and Consciousness*, ed. Jayne Gackenbach, 83–99 (Hauppauge, NY: Nova Science, 2012).

3. A. Tellegen and G. Atkinson, "Openness to Absorbing and Self-Altering Experiences ('Absorption'), a Trait Related to Hypnotic Susceptibility," *Journal of Abnormal Psychology* 83, no. 3 (1974): 268–277, https://doi.org/10.1037/h0036681.

4. David Weibel, Bartholomäus Wissmath, and Fred W. Mast, "Immersion in Mediated Environments: The Role of Personality Traits," *Cyberpsychology, Behavior and Social Networking* 13, no. 3 (2010): 251–256, https://doi.org/10.1089/cyber.2009.0171.

5. Joseph Glicksohn, "Absorption, Hallucinations, and the Continuum Hypothesis," *Behavioral and Brain Sciences* 27, no. 6 (2004): 793–794, https://doi.org/10.1017/S0140525X04280189; Cherise Rosen et al., "Immersion in Altered Experience: An Investigation of the Relationship Between Absorption and Psychopathology," *Consciousness and Cognition* 49 (March 2017): 215–226, https://doi.org/10.1016/j.concog.2017.01.015.

6. Michiel van Elk et al., "The Neural Correlates of the Awe Experience: Reduced Default Mode Network Activity During Feelings of Awe," *Human Brain Mapping* 40, no. 12 (2019): 3561–3574, https://doi.org/10.1002/hbm.24616.

7. Mihaly Csikszentmihalyi, *Flow: The Psychology of Optimal Experience*, 6th ed. (New York: Harper & Row, 1990).

8. M. F. Kaplan and E. Singer, "Dogmatism and Sensory Alienation: An Empirical Investigation," *Journal of Consulting Psychology* 27, no. 6 (1963): 486–491, https://doi.org/10.1037/h0042057; Haylie L. Miller and Nicoleta L. Bugnariu, "Level of Immersion in Virtual Environments Impacts the Ability to Assess and Teach Social Skills in Autism Spectrum Disorder," *Cyberpsychology, Behavior and Social Networking* 19, no. 4 (2016): 246–256, https://doi.org/10.1089/cyber.2014.0682.

Chapter 12: An Optimal Mind for the Occasion

1. Noa Herz, Shira Baror, and Moshe Bar, "Overarching States of Mind," *Trends in Cognitive Sciences* 24, no. 3 (2020): 184–199, https://doi.org/10.1016/j.tics.2019.12.015.

2. W. H. Murray, *The Scottish Himalayan Expedition* (London: J. M. Dent & Sons, 1951), 6–7.

3. Alexei J. Dawes et al., "A Cognitive Profile of Multi-sensory Imagery, Memory and Dreaming in Aphantasia," *Scientific Reports* 10, no. 10022 (2020), https://doi.org/10.1038/s41598-020-65705-7.

4. Ernest G. Schachtel, *Metamorphosis: On the Conflict of Human Development and the Development of Creativity* (New York: Routledge, 2001).

5. Timothy D. Wilson et al., "Social Psychology. Just Think: The Challenges of the Disengaged Mind," *Science* 345, no. 6192 (2014): 75–77, https://doi.org/10.1126/science.1250830.

6. Not to be confused with the Buddhist concept of Emptiness, which pertains more to the detachment from the self and from prejudices and other top-down distortions of perception.

Index